STATLER
THE MAN AND THE MACHINE

Paul Statler
Mildred Statler

Statler by Gammill

25th ANNIVERSARY!

1990 - 2015

STATLER

THE MAN AND THE MACHINE

[signature: David Statler]

25TH ANNIVERSARY EDITION

The inspiring story of Paul Truman Statler
and the invention of his industry changing
computerized quilting machine

DAVID PAUL STATLER

Statler : The Man and The Machine

25th Anniversary Edition

Copyright © 2016 by David Paul Statler
All rights reserved

Printed in the United States of America

ISBN 978-1-48357-807-1

10 9 8 7 6 5 4 3 2 1

First Edition

All rights reserved. No part of this book may be reproduced or transmitted in any form whatsoever without the express written permission of the publisher except for the use of brief quotations in a book review.

Although every precaution has been taken to verify the accuracy of the information contained herein, the author and publisher assume no responsibility for any errors or omissions. No liability is assumed for damages that may result from the use of information contained within.

Trademarks: Gammill, PrecisionStitch, CreativeStudio, Statler Stitcher, Statler by Gammill, and related trade dress are trademarks or registered trademarks of Gammill, Inc. and/or its affiliates in the United States or other countries, and may not be used without written permission. All other trademarks are the property of their respective owners.

Photos were obtained from private family collections.

About the Cover:
Photography by Mary (Statler) Foley.
Cover Design by David Statler, Matt Sherman, and Jared Statler.
The quilt "Serengeti" was created by Kim Diamond and Jo Ann Blade.

Introduction

During a lunch time conversation with my parents, my father brought up the topic of wanting a book written about his life which also told the background story of how the Statler Stitcher came to be. Since it was the 25th anniversary of creating the first Statler machine, it was the perfect time to create such a book. I immediately told him that I wanted to write it and share with readers the wonderful stories I had heard many times.

My father, Paul Statler, grew up on a farm in southeast Missouri with an insatiable thirst to understand how things functioned. He taught himself how to back up a haywagon with a tractor at age six, started his own business of repairing radios and televisions as a teenager, had a satisfying career in the bio-medical technology field, and later created an industry changing computerized longarm quilting machine. Along the way he helped others where he could and encouraged and inspired people with his ingenuity, honesty, integrity, and Christian values.

I have always looked up to my father because of these traits and I am very proud of him. If there was one person I would want with me on a deserted island, it would be my father as I am sure he could create a radio transmitter from coconuts, palm tree leaves, and bamboo.

David P. Statler

"The foundation stones for a balanced success are honesty, character, integrity, faith, love, and loyalty." - Zig Ziglar

Acknowledgments

I would like to thank my father and mother for the opportunity to tell their life stories and to chronicle how his invention of the computerized longarm machine changed the quilting industry.

I would also like to thank my wife and children for their understanding and patience with me while I have been working on this project.

Thanks to my sister, Mary (Statler) Foley, for putting up with me throughout our growing up years, from knock-down fights, arguments, and pranks to sharing the love of video production, computers, and music in our later years.

A special thank you goes out to my aunt, Mary Alice (Statler) Blaylock, for planting, cultivating, and growing my interest in researching our family history.

Many thanks go out to the following people for their editing assistance: Marilyn Logan, Linda Keehn, Matt Sherman, Joseph Bittle, Michelle Weaver, and Shandi Brinkman.

David P. Statler

Foreword

BY DAVID L. JONES

My path first crossed with those of Paul and Mildred Statler at a weekly Bible study when I was a teenager. That Bible study became Christian Chapel in Columbia, Missouri, where I met Angie, whom I married in May of 1986. In the church orchestra, I played the trombone beside a trumpet player named David Statler, and got to know his parents, Paul and Mildred. It was several years later that my wife and I would become close friends with them.

Soon after Angie and I were married, we began going out to eat with Paul and Mildred after Sunday morning church. They invited us to their house for a Sunday meal, and when Mildred fixed her world famous spaghetti, we were hooked. They adopted us, and we spent Sundays for nine years at their house, with our children believing Paul and Mildred were their grandparents. Spending time with the Statlers on Sunday afternoons was especially important for us as a young couple. We got to witness first hand the interaction of a Christ-centered, mature married couple who became important role models for us.

During these Sunday afternoon visits we observed Paul's ingenuity around his home. He was always rigging up something to automate or mechanize a task. Anything to do with electronics, hydraulics, computers, automobiles, machinery or technology equally fascinated us. Regardless of what we were working on, Paul and I both shared mutual interest in our projects, and always enjoyed working together to blend our creative talents on the latest one, whatever that might be. Paul's interest in technology was off the charts. At his age most people would be content in the rocking chair, but not Paul; he had the mind of a teenager.

Paul and Mildred were early adopters of what we know as the Internet. For them, the Internet era began when the University of Missouri first offered their students remote access to an educational network, allowing the opportunity to remotely access the school's data libraries from home computers. This access was later expanded to the community using a free-net concept called C.O.I.N. (Columbia Online Information Network), which also allowed users to send e-mail messages. Paul had already set up an account. Realizing the potential of this new technology, my company partnered with several other communications providers and the educational community to form a network called RAIN (Rural Area Information Network) to bring the first Internet access to rural communities in North Missouri. Any time a new product is rolled out, beta testers are crucial to find the flaws and weaknesses. Paul, with his eagerness to learn and explore new technology, was very willing to test each and every new feature we developed, spending hours on the phone with me looking for holes and glitches in our systems. Angie and Mildred enjoyed a sense of pioneering in the new frontier of e-mail.

Our families enjoyed camping together. At the time, we owned a Winnebago Itasca Phasar, powered by an efficient but ultimately unreliable Renault turbo-diesel. During the course of our ownership, I had to make extensive and continuous use of my mechanical abilities, more than once overhauling the motor due to its unfortunate tendency to overheat at inopportune moments. I also learned to carry a spare alternator, since it was overtaxed and failed frequently. While it was very fuel efficient and fun to travel in, keeping it running eventually became too overwhelming.

Having reached this conclusion on the side of the road yet again, I called Paul and told him I was through with the motor home and its incessant plague of problems. Paul was very interested in the motor home and proceeded to engineer his own version of a "Murphy" system to monitor the engine. When any predetermined limit was reached, the system would automatically adjust parameters to return the engine to safe operation. With Paul's modifications, the dash looked more like an airplane cockpit than a motor home, with annunciator lights and buzzers galore. Paul enjoyed the constant flow of information assuring him the system was operating properly; however it made Mildred very nervous.

Paul and Mildred are an example of a couple where opposites attract. Paul is a very outgoing extroverted person, always eager, motivated, and encouraging. Mildred, a quiet behind the scenes person, is very supportive of most of Paul's adventures, but often acts as the check and balance in their relationship. Together they make an outstanding team, a clear example of a union where two are stronger than one. Mildred is quick to fill in any voids left by Paul.

Paul is what I call a finisher, with the ability to see a project through to completion. This is a trait often lost in today's entrepreneurial business world. Paul often credits me with helping to keep him motivated and encouraged as he worked on developing a computer based quilting machine. I do not think of myself as keeping him motivated, rather I enjoyed the ride along with Paul as he worked to overcome software and hardware obstacles. I remember weeks where the only progress was trying to improve the consistency of stitch lengths while sewing a circle. While the product looked perfectly fine to me, Paul was not happy until the stitch length was exact. He was aware the handcrafting quilt community would not accept anything less. Mildred may have been the one who set the standard, but I can confirm that Paul wanted nothing less than perfection. He realized this was possible with modern computer technology.

I remember when Paul first approached a prominent manufacturer of longarm quilting machines about using a computer to guide his quilting machine. Paul described how his computer could sew in both directions. The manufacturer was adamant that this was not possible. Traditional understanding was that you could only move forward. Trying to sew backward would cause the needle to miss the bobbin and stitches to be lost. What they did not know was that Paul had slightly adjusted the sewing machine and with the precision of computer control was able to sew equally well in both directions. Had Paul accepted conventional wisdom, the Statler Stitcher would never have been born. He understood that when someone says it cannot be done, it just means they do not know how to do it. This is one of the reasons Paul and I bonded. Neither of us can tolerate "it can't be done" solutions.

We are always looking for a way to do it. I am sure the Wright Brothers had much the same philosophy while working to develop the airplane.

One of Paul's strengths is being able to listen to customers and understand their needs. He has the unique ability to understand the operation of hardware while at the same time knowing how to create software to control the hardware. This knowledge gives him the ability to use both to create solutions to solve customers' needs and wants. His understanding of how to market and support these innovative products to customers is what has, in large part, led to the success of Statler Stitcher. I have been with Paul when he personally visited a customer to retrofit a very early machine; rather than force the customer to buy a newer version, he allowed them to continue to use their machine.

I have seen Paul spend hours with customers on the phone, always patient, genuinely caring, and working to solve their problems, whether it was a machine issue, a lack of training, or even if he knew the customer had purchased a cloned machine from another manufacturer. To the customer, it would seem that they were Paul's only responsibility and would support it as if he himself had manufactured it and sold it. This level of support speaks volumes about Paul and his desire to follow Christ. As you read this book you will gain insight into Paul and Mildred Statler. You will come to realize that they are God-gifted people of high integrity who genuinely desire to represent Christ in their daily personal and professional lives.

David L. Jones
Manager
Air Direct, L.L.C.
Powderly, Texas

Table of Contents

PART ONE : THE MAN

Statler Roots 2
The Early Days 6
The Defining Moment 14
Changes and the Dream 16
Behind Every Good Man 22
Love and Marriage 25
Military Life 28
Growing the Family 34
VA in Columbia 42
The Move to Englewood 44
Back in Columbia 48
The Solar Home 50

PART TWO : THE MACHINE

A Dream Come True 60
Automation 63
Partnership 66
First Customers 69
The Guild 71
Star of David Quilt 73
Kim Diamond and the First MQS 76
Changing Hands of the Prototype 79
It is all in the Details 80
Off and Running 82
Special Deliveries 85
Corporate Ownership 87
A New Beginning 89
The Wreck 93
Statler Congress and S.U.G.A.R. 96
The Next Chapter 101

"Bell Star" by Jo Ann Blade and Kim Diamond

PART ONE

STATLER
THE MAN

CHAPTER ONE

Statler Roots

The story of Paul Statler technically begins in the Year of our Lord, Nineteen Hundred and Thirty-Eight. But his true beginnings start long before that. The characteristics that make him who he is today come from the family members that preceded him, passing down not just their DNA, but also their passions, struggles, determination, perseverance, ideologies, and faith in God.

To gain a better understanding of the family's origins, Paul's sister, Mary Alice (Statler) Blaylock, has been researching the family genealogy for over 40 years and has documented the Statler (originally spelled Stadler) family stretching back 400 years to the 1600's. She discovered family ancestors who made the first voyage from Germany to America on the ship "Alexander and Anne," which docked at port in Philadelphia, Pennsylvania on September 5, 1730. She then followed their descendants through the decades from Shade Township, Somerset County, Pennsylvania to Lincolnton, Lincoln County, North Carolina when land was given to Statler Revolutionary War soldiers as payment for their service. In the fall of 1799, after the harvest was brought in, brothers Peter and Conrad Statler, along with their families, friends, and neighbors, loaded up what belongings would fit in their wagons and headed west toward the promise of a better future.

Malachi Hasting Statler

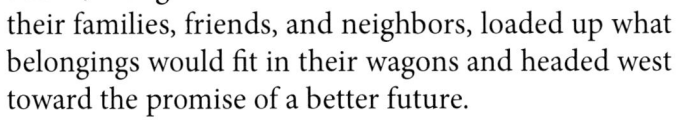

There are no documented writings of their journey, so we can only imagine what hardships they faced during the trip. Crossing the Great Smoky Mountains in the Appalachians by wagon would almost seem like an impossible task just by itself. What only takes about ten hours by car today took approximately five months by wagon train.

Bertha Alice Statler

Family lore states that these families crossed a frozen Mississippi River on New Year's Day of 1800 into the area now known as Ste. Genevieve, Missouri. After arriving, they most likely had to wait out the rest of winter, restocked the supplies, and then head south to settle in Bollinger and Cape Girardeau counties, where they obtained land grants from the Spanish government. They then began the backbreaking work of clearing the land, building houses and barns, and getting the fields ready for planting.

At the end of 1803, with the Louisiana Purchase transaction, the families were now once again living in the United States.

From one of the Bollinger County Statler branches was born Paul's grandfather, Miller Malachi Hastings Statler. Malachi, or "Chi" as he was known, was the son of Jesse Christian Statler and Mary Ann Seabaugh. Chi married Bertha Alice "Allie" Statler, a 3rd cousin, on December 15, 1907 in Sedgewickville, Missouri. Allie's parents were Peter Amos Statler and Sarah Elizabeth Bowers.

Chi and Bertha Alice Statler Wedding Photo - 1907

Chi and Allie had four children: Della Mae, Carrie Edna, Coy Truman, and Thurman Gifford. Coy Truman Statler, Paul's father, was born February 27, 1915 in Sedgewickville. Coy and his siblings grew up on the farm, doing the daily chores required of youngsters, attending a one-room schoolhouse and learning the ways of becoming a farmer like their father. At the age of four, Coy suffered a bout of rheumatic fever which left him with a heart murmur that he suffered with for the rest of his life.

Statler Family - About 1921
Coy, Della, Bertha, and Carrie
Malachi holding Thurman

Allie, Paul's grandmother, had always loved music and wanted to own an organ. In her mid-twenties, she began a small business of growing, picking, and selling garden peas to save up enough money to buy one. Close to the time of her marriage in 1907, she finally had enough money saved and ordered a Windsor brand parlor style harmonium (commonly referred to as a "pump organ") from the Sears and Roebuck catalog at the cost of $60. Her father took the horse-drawn wagon to pick up the organ when it arrived by train at the Jackson, Missouri station. The organ was operated by pressing petals by foot which created a vacuum. When the keys were played, air blew across reeds to create the sound. After teaching herself to play, she began playing the church's organ during services.

When the small Trinity Methodist Church where she and Chi attended bought a new organ, Allie was the first to play it.

Bohnenkamp Family
Earl, Mildred, May, Amy, Samuel
Lucy, Marvin, Henry, Clara

Coy Truman Statler
1928 - Age 13

Paul still has the old pump organ his grandmother worked so hard to buy. His children had their first music lessons on it, sitting on the lap of their grandmother, Paul's mother, Mildred, who would pump the organ while teaching the children. Paul also recently purchased the old Trinity Church's W.W. Kimball pump organ that his grandmother played.

In October of 1933, the Bohnenkamp family moved to Sedgewickville when the Rev. Samuel David Bohnenkamp was appointed as the new minister of the United Methodist Church. Rev. Bohnenkamp and his wife Amy Eva Sites had seven children: Alice May, Mildred Marie, Earl Austin, Clara Amy, Henry Edward, Marvin Herman, and Lucy Thelma. Mildred Marie Bohnenkamp, Paul's mother, was born February 21, 1916 in Bourbon, Missouri.

Since they attended the same church, Coy and Mildred quickly became friends and courtship was not far behind. They were married in the United Methodist Church in Sedgewickville on October 9, 1935, not long after the Great Depression and right in the height of the Dust Bowl era. It

Mildred Marie Bohnenkamp
High School Graduation Photo - 1933

was reported to have been the largest wedding held in the church at the time. Coy and Mildred started their new life together on a nearby farm and began making the land their own.

It wasn't long before their first child, Mary Alice, was born on August 1, 1936. That was also the year that their barn burned down, possibly due to "green" hay which was stored in the barn too soon. Almost two years later, her brother Paul Truman was born.

At the end of 1941, the United States entered the conflict of World War II. Coy was drafted into military service, but due to recovering from a very bad case of pneumonia, he was too sick to go. His heart murmur was probably another condition that affected his draft status. Not to be deterred from serving his country, he decided to pack up his family and move to St. Louis to find work.

Coy and Mildred Statler Wedding Photo - 1935

Mary Alice Statler 1937 - Age 1

As Coy's parents aged, health problems mounted and it was becoming more difficult for them to work and keep up their farm. Allie suffered with stomach ailments and Chi developed heart problems. Paul believes that this is one of the major reasons that they retired from farming in the 1940s. Around the end of 1942, Coy was asked by his parents to take over the Statler family farm operations. Moving back from St. Louis, he gladly took over the responsibility of caring and cultivating the 200 acres of land and raising his young family. Chi and Allie moved into a smaller farmhouse about a mile from the original farm, raising a few calves and hogs and always planting a small garden.

Malichi and Bertha Alice Statler

5

CHAPTER TWO

The Early Days

Paul Truman Statler was born at home on the family farm on July 11, 1938 in the small Missouri boot-heel town of Sedgewickville, Missouri, the second child of Coy and Mildred Bohnenkamp Statler, joining his two year old sister Mary Alice.

Some of Paul's earliest memories are from when his family was still living in St. Louis. His sister Mary Alice, five years old at the time, better remembers the air-raid sirens going off, having to cover the windows to block out the lights and the street lights going off. The family only stayed in St. Louis about a year before they left and headed back home to Sedgewickville when Coy took over the multi-generational Statler family farm.

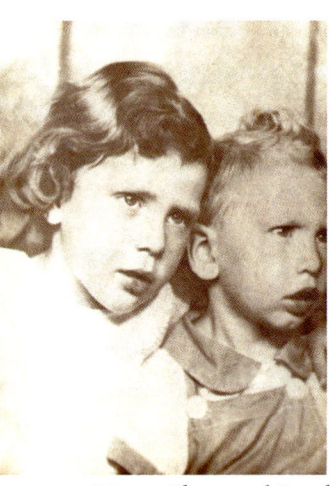

Mary Alice and Paul

One early memory that stands out for Paul was his fear of the farm animals, even the chickens. Naturally, for a small four-year old, a large cow would seem quite intimidating, but his mother would continually bring him up close to the animals to help him overcome his fear. Around that same time, Paul would witness his father milking the cows and wanted to give it a try. Not wanting to squash his interest and enthusiasm, but

Mildred, Coy, and Paul in front of the farm house

6

being mindful of Paul's hesitancy around animals, Coy taught him how to milk the goats instead, something more his size.

Paul riding along with his father Coy on the Farmall tractor

Paul's father used horses for the farm work until he bought his first tractor, a Farmall Type B, in 1944. Being around the horses allowed Paul to figure out how their harnesses were hooked up. Using some rope, Paul rigged up a small harness for the goats, which he attached to his little red wagon and had them pull him around the farm.

In the early days on the farm there were few conveniences. There was no electricity, no indoor plumbing for running water or toilets, no air conditioning, no refrigerator or freezer to keep food fresh. Paul's mother had to can just about everything, including beef, to preserve their food. Other food items like potatoes and apples were stored under haystacks in a dry area for safe keeping even though Paul would occasionally dig through the hay to snack on an apple. As with most households at that time, the "restroom" was an outhouse somewhere in the backyard away from the main house. The family used a bucket at night to keep from having to make the trip in the dark, which was then promptly emptied in the morning. Kerosene lamps lit the house at night and wood was used for cooking and heat.

Statler Family
Mildred, Coy, Paul, and Mary Alice

"Running water" usually consisted of Paul getting a bucket of water from the cistern out near the back porch. For quite awhile, he thought his middle name was "get a bucket of water" because every time he heard his name called, it was always followed by "get a bucket of water." The cistern was a hole in the ground lined with rocks and sealed with concrete. Rainwater would run off the roof of the house into the hole to collect a small water supply. There was also a natural spring nearby, so Paul would occasionally get his bucket of water from the spring. In 1950, when Paul was twelve years old, the Rural Electric Association finally brought electricity to those living outside of town. One of the first things they did was put an electric pump at the spring to run fresh water to the house.

Mary Alice and Paul

Education was very important to Paul's parents, especially his mother Mildred. She had earned a teaching degree from Southeast Missouri State University in Cape Girardeau, Missouri before she had married and even taught in the one-room schoolhouse where Paul and Mary Alice attended. Paul was held back a year by his mother to wait for a larger class of first graders. He was grateful for having more classmates his age, and since reading and writing were not his strongest subjects, it helped in repeating some of the lessons.

The schoolhouse was one of the farming community's main gathering places for town hall meetings and of course learning the "Three R's". In December of 1942, the Statler family

Mildred with her students at the Limbaugh School
Mary Alice is on the far left, second row
Paul is in the front, far right, wearing the sweater

8

attended a Christmas function held at the local one-room schoolhouse. "Santy" Claus, as Paul says it, was at the party helping to bring smiles to the children. A local preacher in attendance was making a disruption about not liking Santy Claus. Because Paul's father was on the school board, he asked the preacher to leave the party. Because Paul was only four and still believed in Santy Claus at the time, his father thought the schoolhouse was for a safe learning place and not the place for discovering about the existence of Santy Claus.

Paul, along with his sister, had to walk about a mile each day to and from school. When his mother taught at the school, she would walk along with them. It always seemed like a long walk to him and a struggle to keep up with the bigger kids. During the really cold winter days, his mother would wrap his shoes in layers of newspaper to keep his feet warmer on the long walk. When snow was deeper than the tops of his shoes, feed sacks would be wrapped around his shoes and legs.

Mary Alice and Paul with their maternal grandparents, Sam and Amy Bohnenkamp

When Paul was about six years old, his Aunt Clara gave him a toy tractor as a present. Not being completely happy with it because he couldn't turn the front wheels, he made a few "modifications" to it so he could steer it. This was about the same time when his father bought his first tractor for the farm. Coy was continually having problems backing the connected wagon into the barn. Paul hooked up a little wagon to his toy tractor and practiced backing it up. His father was so impressed and confident in Paul's skills that he let him drive the tractor and back the wagon into the barn. He was only six years old! Paul looks at six year olds today and wonders what his dad was thinking!

It was also around this time when Paul's father took him squirrel hunting. When the squirrel was within range, Coy handed the shotgun to his young son and he shot the small animal dead. Being sensitive to all living creatures, Paul decided right then that he would never again shoot another animal, and he hasn't.

Paul and Mary Alice Statler

The Statler farm had a lot of animals that required feeding every day, along with milking the cows and goats. Coy awoke his children at 4 a.m. every day to get all the chores

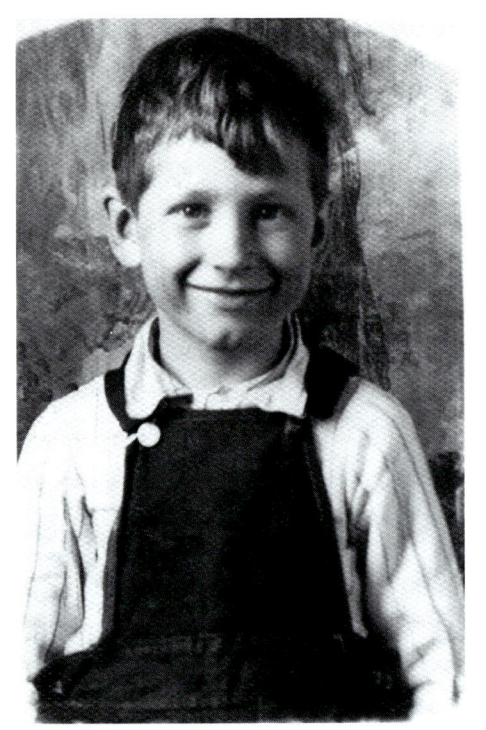

Paul Statler

done before having to walk to school. After school, there were always more chores awaiting them.

One aspect of farm life that Paul did not like was the killing of the animals. They had goats on the farm because the doctor said goat's milk would be good for Paul's grandmother, but occasionally there were times when Coy had to kill one of them. He would hang it up by its hind feet and then slit the throat allowing it to bleed out. Ice water would then be poured into the carcass to quickly cool the meat. It may not have been an enjoyable process, but it was necessary sometimes for food.

Paul did not like the killing of chickens either, but there was one mean rooster that would constantly jump on his back, digging in his claws and spurs, and flog him by flapping his wings. After the corn was harvested, any remaining corn stalks would be cut off using a long corn knife. As Paul would bend over to use the knife on the stalks, this rooster took advantage of the opportunity to jump on his back and flog him. The rooster would try this on Coy as well, but he would turn around and kick him hard with his boot. This tactic did not work for Paul since he was smaller and therefore became an easy target. After witnessing this a few times, Coy told his young son, "You've got a weapon in your hand." The next time the mean rooster attacked, Paul swung around real fast and using the corn knife, chopped off his head. He then grabbed up the rooster by the legs so it would bleed out and headed to the house. When Paul's mother saw him coming, she came out and said, "Good! I needed something to cook for supper." It was the suffering of the animals that really bothered Paul, but he had no regrets in killing this rooster and it did not suffer for one minute.

Another part of farming that was not so enjoyable was mending fences. After every storm, about 10 miles of fence line had to be examined for broken wire or fallen branches. The fences were important to protect the animals and to keep them on the property.

Mildred and Coy Statler

What Paul did love about farming was learning how all of the equipment worked and seeing the advancements as they came out.

Limbaugh School, Sedgewicksville, Missouri

The old one-room schoolhouse Paul attended closed after his sixth grade year. Paul's father was on the school board at the time and the decision was made to have all of the small schools in the area consolidate into Sedgewickville, Missouri. From his seventh grade year through the tenth, Paul still had to walk a mile each day to catch a bus into town for school.

Paul mostly enjoyed school, but there was a time when he endured some teasing and bullying by some of the older kids. He had just moved to the recently consolidated school in Sedgewickville and drew the attention of some of the girls. Since he was smaller in stature as a young boy, one of the larger boys kept pushing and shoving him and making fun of him because he was jealous of Paul. Talking to his father, Paul was told that he should find a way to stop him if he could. That got him to thinking of a way. Each time Paul was tripped or shoved, he would say to him, "You'd better stop that or I'm going to hurt you!" The bully was a lot larger, but Paul was stronger from lifting hay bales almost as big as he was. The taunting went on for quite a while which gave Paul time to figure out how to put a stop to it. Then the fateful day came. After pushing Paul around once more, the kid turned to walk away, feeling smug and proud. Paul grabbed him by the shoulders, spun him

Paul Statler

around, and punched him as hard as he could in the face. Being caught off guard and off balance, the boy fell to the ground. Paul jumped on top of him, slamming his knees into the boy's arm muscles, and began to hit him over and over in the face. The other boys standing around watching the ordeal had to pull Paul off. Paul's dad had said to teach him a lesson if he could, and Paul was apparently a good teacher as the kid never bothered him again after that. It happened one other time with another boy and Paul taught him the same lesson as well. He was never bullied after that. Puberty hit later that summer helping Paul grow six inches so he was no longer one of the small kids.

Paul's unquenchable thirst for knowledge and discovery drove him to uncover the mysteries of how things were built and functioned. Once while driving the farm tractor, one of the wheels drove over some ice while the other wheel stayed on gravel. The wheel on the slick ice began spinning twice as fast while the wheel in the gravel stopped turning and Paul wondered why. An old Model-T automobile that belonged to Paul's grandfather was still on the farm, so Paul took off the cover plate to the differential to figure out how the gears worked. After seeing how it was all put together, it all made sense of how differential gears helped vehicles and tractors turn corners.

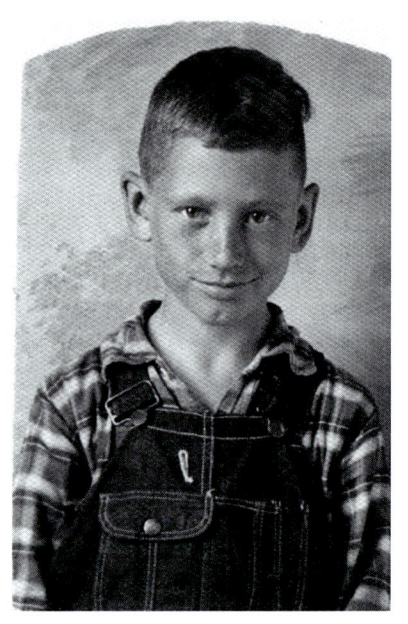

Paul Statler

A few years after this discovery, Paul's science teacher was presenting the function of a differential, but was not getting it quite right. After some discussion with the teacher, it was clear he still did not understand it, so Paul felt the need to demonstrate it to him. He asked his father to drive the farm truck into town where Paul showed the teacher how if you jack up the truck and do not allow one of the wheels to turn, the other one will spin twice as fast, just as the tractor reacted on the ice. The science teacher was surprised that one of his students understood something better than he did, but Paul thought he should not be teaching something incorrectly. Another time they got into a discussion about electrical generators. Paul demonstrated that to get electrical power from a generator, mechanical power must be put into it.

Mildred and Coy Statler

Even though Paul's father was first and foremost a farmer, he kept very busy during the off-season. Coy ran a sawmill on some property he had purchased a mile from the farm, cutting siding planks for neighbors' barns, 2x4's and 2x6's, etc. One year, someone started siphoning off the gasoline from the sawmill engine. In an attempt to catch the thief, Coy replaced the gas in the tank with water. Sure enough the next morning, the "gas" had once again been removed from the tank, and the culprit's car was found a short time later on the side of the road.

Coy also dealt with a chicken thief. Chickens had begun disappearing from the chicken house during the night. To alert himself and to scare the thief during his next attempt, he mounted a shotgun pointed away from the door and attached a string between the gun's trigger and the doorknob. Close to two o'clock in the morning, a loud shot rang out. After jumping out of bed and looking through the window on the moonlit night, the whole family got a big laugh at how fast the thief was running away through the fields. They never lost any more chickens after that.

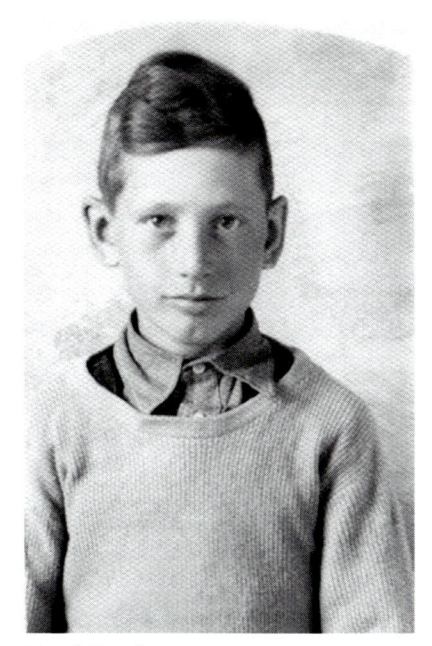

Paul Statler

When Paul was 13 years old, he along with three other teenagers and his sister Mary Alice, were traveling to a church youth event in Patton, Missouri. The driver of the car, a newly-licensed 16 year old girl was driving a little too fast and lost control of the car going around a curve. Paul was riding in the middle of the back seat and during one of the flips of the car, the back glass popped out and he was thrown out. Even though they were not wearing seat belts, thankfully no one was seriously injured. Paul walked away with some bad scrapes and cuts, requiring stitches in the back of his head and a lasting scar by his nose.

Paul pulling the wagon

CHAPTER THREE

The Defining Moment

Paul believes that his father's interest in keeping up with the progress of farming equipment was very influential in his own life. It seemed like an easy shift from understanding the mechanics of farm equipment to a lifetime fascination with electronics. Paul remembers to this day the defining moment of discovering what he wanted to do the rest of his life.

Around 1947 when Paul was about 9, he passed by the doctor's office while walking through town one day and saw something through the open door that he had only read about before. It was a new television set playing a show which was being broadcast out of St. Louis, Missouri. It was a glorious sight to behold!

A few years after this encounter, and still before they had electricity at the farm, Paul and family were visiting some friends of his father. They lived closer to town and already had electricity at their house. The friend's television set had been taken apart with the tubes, other components, and the main picture tube all sitting out on the kitchen table for repair. As soon as Paul saw this, he knew in his heart that this was what he wanted to do.

While in his tenth grade year, Paul discussed with his father an interest in taking correspondence classes in electronics. He had seen an advertisement in a mechanical magazine and Coy agreed to help get him started. The classes in television and radio repair were offered through the DeVry Technical Institute. Paul sold a calf he had raised and his father agreed to cover the rest of the tuition.

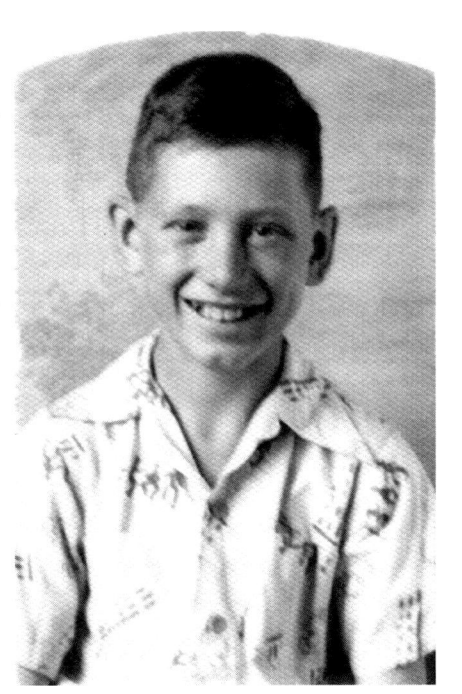

Paul Statler

The lessons were on 16mm film rolls which Paul watched by hand cranking a projector loaned to him by the Institute. Engrossed by what he saw, he watched the film lessons over and over, learning how electronic circuits formed, how electrons moved through a vacuum tube, how to assemble parts on a chassis, and on and on. Each month another assignment and film lesson would arrive to try and fulfill Paul's hunger for learning in this exciting new world of electronics. Paul built all of the testing equipment he used based on the various assignments and film lessons.

The electronics field was changing so frequently that DeVry sent an entire new set of updated textbooks because of it. When Paul began the course, only vacuum tubes were being used, which took a lot of energy to run and got very hot to the touch. Solid-state transistors eventually took their place which used less energy and stayed cool. Paul continually had to learn these changes in technology to keep up throughout his entire life.

The final project in the correspondence course was building an actual television set. Each lesson focused on a particular function of a television which Paul would build, like the power supply, the radio-frequency (RF) tuner and receiver, how to wire sockets for vacuum tubes, etc. After each test, he would return the film lesson and the school would send another one which instructed Paul how to build the next section. The last part to complete the project was the television's main picture tube. Paul rode with his father to the train station in Poplar Bluff, Missouri, which was about 80 miles away, to pick it up as that was the closest place DeVry would ship.

Returning home, Paul could hardly wait to install the final part of his masterpiece. Finally, it was completed and the moment of truth had arrived. He turned it on and—nothing but static! He then realized it was 2 a.m. and the television stations did not start their broadcasting day until 6 a.m.! It was a long four hours, but what excitement ensued during the glorious presentation of the National Anthem beaming through the new television set! Paul even built the cabinet for the set in shop class at school and it was used many years as the main family television in the home.

Paul and the television set he built

After this successful endeavor, Paul began repairing other people's televisions and radios in and around the community. Coming full circle, he even repaired the television of the doctor that he saw through the open door that one life-changing day.

CHAPTER FOUR

Changes and the Dream

Paul's parents were very spiritually oriented. They attended church every weekend and read the Bible each evening. Coy even studied to preach as a lay person for their church or at one of the smaller churches nearby. He really enjoyed it and filled the pulpit quite often when the pastor was out circuit preaching. Paul remembers his father reading the Bible by the kitchen cook stove to stay warm in the winter and his mother reading to the whole family by the light of the kerosene lamp.

Paul and his mother Mildred

When Paul was fifteen in 1953, his father, at age 38, announced that he was going to attend seminary to become a full-time preacher due to his obedience to a calling from the Lord. Paul is confident that his parents thought and prayed about it a lot before announcing this life change to him and his sister.

It seemed like everything Paul was involved with, whether it was farming or electronics, continually changed, so the announcement of his father leaving did not seem like a big shock to him. He took on his father's chores before he left for seminary and even though it added to his workload, Paul does not remember it being a tougher time, being scared or even finding it unusual. Life just went on with a reliance on God for guidance and provision.

Over the next two years Coy attended seminary located at Southern Methodist University in Dallas, Texas. His soon to be son-in-law Donald Blaylock and brother-in-law Andy Fowler also attended, each studying to enter the ministry. Paul's mother even attended a few classes.

Despite the added workload, Paul took the time to play pranks on his sister. One time, before she arrived back home from a date with her then boyfriend, Donald Blaylock, Paul used quite a bit of hay baling wire to tie the gate shut. Unfortunately, Donald had a pair of wire cutters in his car. Another time he tied a long string to the porch light string puller and attached it to the gate. When Mary Alice's boyfriend opened the gate, the porch light came on and Paul cranked the record player which began blaring the song, *"Give Me More, More, More of Your Kisses"* by William Orville "Lefty" Frizzell.

In 1954, Paul turned sixteen and he distinctly remembers the day he obtained his driver's license. Even though he drove just about everything around the farm, because he did not have his license, his father would not allow him to drive on the roads. His mother took him to Marble Hill, Missouri, which was the county seat in Bollinger County and after passing the test to get his license, she let him drive home. He was so excited to get to drive on the public roads.

The Statlers, circa 1954

It was also during this time that Paul's sister, Mary Alice, married Donald Blaylock on June 5, 1954 at the Sedgewickville United Methodist Church.

Mary Alice Statler and Donald Blaylock Wedding Photo - 1954

Once Coy had finished seminary and was credentialed in the early spring of 1955, he returned home, packed up their belongings, and moved with Paul's mother to take over the Methodist church in Lowndes, Missouri. Because Paul only had a few months of school left before summer break, he stayed at home on the farm. During what spare hours he had, he mostly worked on his correspondence courses.

Once school was over, Paul joined his parents in Lowndes and the farm was sold. In addition to the Methodist church in Lowndes, Paul's father also preached at three

Paul and his mother Mildred in front of the house in Lowndes, Missouri

17

other small country churches as part of his circuit. Paul's mother was also a very important part of the ministry. She would often play the piano or organ, and would usually lead the singing. Coy was not much of a singer, but would occasionally lead a hymn. Paul never played an instrument, but did sing in a quartet as a teenager. His sister Mary Alice also sang and played the piano at church.

Paul attended different schools in his junior and senior years of high school. In his junior year he attended school in Greenville, Missouri. In his senior year he went to school in Zalma, Missouri and was elected Prom King. In the photos taken of him and the Prom Queen, his mother did not approve of how low her dress was in the front and used colored pencils to "raise" the neck line.

Paul as a High School Junior 1955-56

Zalma High School Prom Queen and King - 1957

The Statlers lived in the Lowndes church parsonage which was located next to the general store. The store's owner had two children, Jim and Jeanette Gibbons, who both became close friends with Paul. Jim was also very interested in electronics and Paul learned quite a bit from him. In the summer after Paul's junior year, they constructed an AM radio broadcast station using a radio frequency test generator as the oscillator and modulator, and used a chassis from an old tube-type radio for the linear amplifier. They used Coy's reel-to-reel tape recorder for their source of music. Once they recorded a fictitious weather forecast predicting a heavy snowstorm in the middle of July, due to recent atomic bomb testing. When the forecast was played over the general store's radio, the loafers hanging out there began quite a discourse. One of the men was quoted saying, "By golly, did you hear that?" Paul's radio station used the call letters "KSTP" which stood for "Statler Truman Paul." Paul would broadcast his father's sermons so that if anyone was unable to attend church, they could still hear the sermon.

Paul and Jim Gibbons

After Jim Gibbons graduated high school and left for college, Paul and Jim's sister Jeanette became very good friends, like a brother and sister would be, and did a lot of things together. Paul even taught her how to drive.

A school teacher who lived in Lowndes taught in Zalma, Missouri, which was about 15 miles away. Because her son, who had graduated and left home, was no longer available to drive her to work, Paul was "volunteered." Therefore he transferred to the school in Zalma which is where he graduated from high school. One of the churches on Coy's circuit was in Zalma which is probably how he found out about the teacher's need for a driver. It did not matter to Paul's parents or to himself where he finished school, just that he graduate, which he did. Paul also loved the extra responsibility of driving his teacher to school each day.

Jeanette Gibbons

Paul's father made a lot of improvements to the parsonage house in Lowndes. He converted one of the bedrooms in to a new kitchen and built new kitchen cabinets, installed running water, put a commode in the house, and installed an electric pump on the well.

Paul's mother Mildred in her new kitchen

Like his father, Paul was always tinkering and building things. While living in Lowndes, he read about a parabolic reflector. The article really piqued his interest and he just had to build one. A parabolic reflector is similar to a satellite dish made of folded thin metal about two feet in diameter. It can receive or transmit sounds over a long distance in a narrow straight line. Paul would scare away stray dogs transmitting a tone that only they heard.

He also hooked it up to an audio box that could generate high-pitched sounds. The volume could be controlled by a knob on the box. Once he pointed the reflector towards the woods behind his house and later learned that a hunter had heard the sounds. Besides just sending out annoying frequencies, Paul hooked up a microphone to the center of the reflector to pick up sounds as well. He usually pointed it towards the general store next door from his bedroom window to listen in on the latest gossip.

Not long after moving to Lowndes, Paul began having a recurring dream that he would experience over the next few decades. He wonders if the dream started because he was spending a lot of time finishing his correspondence courses building and repairing television sets and radios. While on the farm, there was always a lot of work and chores to do, but now that he lived in town, he could really concentrate on his interests.

The dream began with Paul walking on a sidewalk between two buildings. In the concrete sidewalk, there was a hole that he had to walk around or fall into. He saw that one of the buildings had an electrical conduit running up its side and there were hot water pipes used for water which was heated by a wood stove. After entering the building, Paul noticed a lot of equipment, tools, mechanical saws, and milling tools of which many of them seemed familiar. There was one special piece of equipment, a welder, that he had never seen before and it puzzled him. Remembering this welder after awakening, he would try to describe it to people, but they did not know what kind it was either.

In 1957, Paul graduated from high school in Zalma, Missouri. Soon after, his father was assigned to the Methodist church in Cardwell, Missouri so the family packed up their belongings once again and headed to their new home in Cardwell.

Now 18 and having gained experience repairing radios and televisions back in Lowndes for family and friends, Paul felt confident to open up his own television and radio repair shop. Having completed his correspondence courses, he had already built voltmeters, oscilloscopes, generators, and all of the other test equipment he needed. A man who attended church where Paul's father preached owned a storefront downtown that had become

20

available and offered it to Paul for no rent the first month. Paul's father Coy traded in the old farm pickup truck for a Willys Jeep station wagon so that televisions would not get wet during deliveries.

Left: Paul working in his new shop   *Right: Paul with his Jeep delivery wagon*

Due to spending most of his time working on the farm, going to school, taking correspondence courses, and running his electronics repair business, there was not a lot of time left to think about girls. Besides his sister, the only other female he spent any time with was Jeannette Gibbons from Lowndes, but she was more like a friend or sister than a romantic interest.

While in Cardwell, a local girl became interested in Paul. She would come by and clean up his shop without asking and do other little odd jobs to try to get his attention. Paul asked a friend at church what he thought of her. He said that she was "a little too friendly, if you know what I mean." It was around Christmas time when she was at the shop putting up Christmas decorations that Paul finally told her that he wasn't interested in her.

Paul standing in front of his shop in downtown Cardwell, MO with Christmas decorations in the window

Sometime later, Paul became interested in another girl that attended his church. She was a little too forward though and he later found out that she was pregnant. Both of these experiences discouraged Paul to the point where he was about to give up on the dating scene altogether.

As it turned out, one day while on an errand to obtain some blank checks at the bank for his shop, Paul met someone who would change the rest of his life. She was a teller at the bank and her name was Mildred Arlene Blansett.

CHAPTER FIVE

Behind Every Good Man

It has always been said that behind every good man is a great woman, and in Paul's case, it is more than a saying, it is the truth.

Mildred Arlene Blansett was born July 2, 1933 at her maternal grandparents' home in Ravenden Springs, Arkansas to Millard Darlin and Zula "Arlene" Bailey Blansett. Her brother, Jewel Leon Blansett, was born three years later on September 11, 1936.

Some of Mildred's earliest memories are reading to her paternal grandmother, Sarah Jane (Smith) Blansett. Mildred was only eight or nine years old at the time when her grandmother became ill and reading to her was a way to keep her company. Mildred was able to pass both the third and fourth grades in one year. She thinks either this was due to her interest in reading or a way to get out of walking the long mile to the one-room schoolhouse as much. Sarah Jane died a few years later in 1945.

Mildred (right) with her cousin, Thurman Wells

Mildred's parents were sharecroppers who rented their farm land. Besides planting corn and beans, the crop they relied on most was cotton.

Mildred's paternal grandparents, William and Sarah Jane Blansett

When Mildred was in the fifth grade, around the year 1942, she and her family moved to the small farming community of Cardwell, Missouri, not far across the border from Arkansas, where the flat, sandy, and loose soil was good for growing cotton. Mildred's father, Millard, would plant the cotton seed every year around Mother's Day, usually when the danger of the spring frosts were over. Once the seedlings were 4-5 inches tall, Millard would declare it was time to "chop the cotton." Chopping cotton was vital to obtaining a good crop. The seedlings had to be thinned out so the more hardy ones would survive. Everyone in the family, along with hired-hands, had to hoe the rows to loosen

SCHOOL DAYS
1943-44

the topsoil to help the small cotton plants to grow. The crops also depended upon a good mix of rain and sun. Too much rain would cause the cotton to turn yellow.

In late summer, the leaves on the cotton plants turned brown and the fields became snowy white when the cotton burst forth from their protective shells, which are called bolls. Now came time for the grueling task of "pickin' cotton" by hand. Mildred would wear gloves with the tips of the fingers cut off to pick cotton and would try every position possible to try helping endure the pain of an eleven hour day. She would pick by either constantly bending over or walking on her knees until the hot sand would burn them, causing her to have to stand and bend over again. She pulled a large sack behind her which she filled with the picked cotton and the sack's constant catching on prickly bolls caused much frustration.

Mildred's father, Millard Blansett

According to Mildred, it seemed that her brother Jewel was always daydreaming or being distracted by every bird and plane that flew over the field. Somehow unbeknownst to her, he was always able to pick a full sack of cotton.

During harvest time, schools used what was called a "split term" to accommodate the farmers needing their children's help in the fields. Even though there were still the regular chores of washing, ironing, and even cooking, they all had to wait until after the picking of the cotton. "Round steak," as Mildred's parents called it, which were slices from a whole stick of bologna, on a slice of bread was what they ate for sandwiches. A few times Mildred would just be too tired to eat and went to bed without dinner. Once the dew was dried on the fields the next morning, it was time for another long hot day's work.

Jewel and Mildred

Early in Mildred's life she learned the lesson of working hard and earning a wage. She was paid by the hour to hoe in the fields and during harvest time, she was paid by the pound of cotton picked. Mildred got to keep some of her pay for spending money and some was kept by her parents to help pay for school clothes.

During the winter, the temperature inside the Blansett's small two-bedroom farmhouse was sometimes just as cold as it was outside, especially when the coal-fueled stove died down during the night. The bucket of water in the kitchen would freeze and the family slept under multiple heavy quilts. Mildred slept in a small room off the kitchen and her brother Jewel slept in the same room with his parents. Mildred remembers it being hard to turn over underneath the weight of the quilts and still not being warm enough. Usually after dinner, Mildred would help her mother in the making of the quilts by cutting the fabric using cardboard templates made from cracker boxes and by sewing the pieces together by hand. Arlene would then quilt the pieced material which was mounted in a frame that was hung from the bedroom ceiling when not in use. These quilts were made not for show or to sell, but were made to keep the family warm on long winter nights.

Finances were very tight for the Blansett family and Mildred does not remember how her parents paid the rent, but she does remember them being very frugal and cautious in their spending. The whole year's income was dependent upon the harvest. Some years the crops would fail, which created a real hardship. Saving money meant survival. Money was spent on the usual things like salt, sugar, hamburger, dry goods, and the occasional roast.

Millard and Arlene Blansett

Mildred remembers her mother sewing all of her clothes. If there was a dress Mildred liked, her mother would buy the pattern and material, but then creatively combine two or three other patterns together to make a unique dress.

Millard was not a very religious person and did not attend church very often, but did live by the Golden Rule, strongly believing in treating others the way he wanted to be treated and teaching his kids to be honest and work hard. Arlene took Mildred and Jewel to church, but they could only get there by riding with Millard's sister Nettie to the local Baptist church where she was a member. Mildred was later baptized in the church while a senior in high school.

SCHOOL DAYS 1947-48

After graduating high school in 1950, Mildred began working at Estel's Drugstore for about a year until an opening for a teller became available at the Cardwell State Bank. One day a handsome young man came in to the bank needing some blank checks for his business. His name was Paul Truman Statler.

Mildred's graduation photo 1950

24

CHAPTER SIX

Love and Marriage

When Paul came in for his blank checks, Mildred stated she did not have any at the counter and had to go back to the storeroom to retrieve some. Her willingness to help him made quite an impression and the fact that she was very pretty helped too. After that, Paul would always come to her teller window to do his banking business.

Paul could not stop thinking about this girl at the bank. She even had the same name as his mother. A revival was going on at the Baptist church and Paul saw Mildred in attendance. He came over and sat down by her. When the service was over, he asked to take her home, but she refused saying she had to drive her mother home. As Paul watched from a distance, he witnessed Mildred getting into the passenger side of the car. Paul then concluded that Mildred just was not interested in dating him so he dropped the thought of pursuing her. A few days later, a man who worked at the bank told Paul that Mildred was definitely interested, and that he should pay more attention to her.

Mildred would get her hair done each week in a salon located next door to Paul's repair shop. The owner of the salon also played matchmaker in trying to fix them up together. Eventually, Paul worked up enough courage to ask Mildred out and she agreed to a date. Their first date was to a basketball game at the high school.

Mildred and Paul in Cardwell, Missouri

One of Millard's rules for dating Mildred was that she had to be home by 11 p.m. On one particular date, things were going smoothly and Paul was going to get Mildred home on time. What he did not expect was the train coming through town making them wait at the crossing. Having to wait on the long train caused him to get his date home past the curfew deadline. At least that is the excuse Paul told Mildred's father.

After a year of dating, Paul nervously proposed, she graciously accepted, and they were married on February 22, 1959 in the Cardwell Baptist church.

Wedding Party
Jewel Blansett, Best Man - June Sikes, Maid of Honor
Ceremony performed by Reverend Cliff Robertson

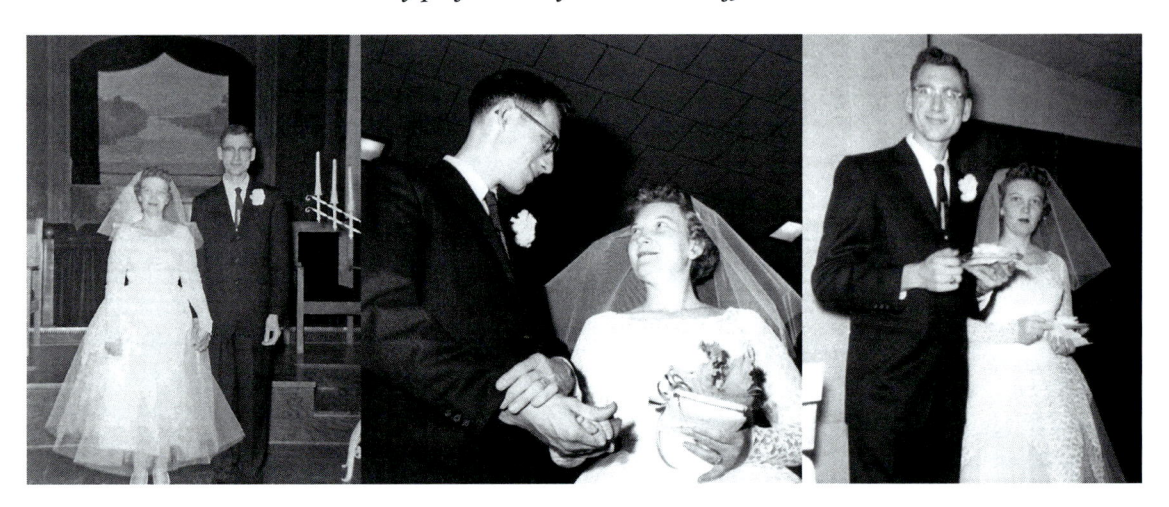

Paul and Mildred made a conscious effort to live frugally and in doing so were able to save enough money from his radio and television business to buy an older car with cash and to pay off their home mortgage (their first home cost $3,000). One way they saved money was that Paul fixed his own cars and they also deposited in savings the amount they would have made in a car payment.

Paul and Mildred's first home in Cardwell
Photo taken in 1990

Paul rigged up a Citizens Band (CB) radio so that he could communicate with Mildred at home from his repair shop. One day a lady told Paul, "I know what you had for dinner last night. I heard it on my television." That was a shock to Paul and somewhat embarrassing, so to fix the problem, he put a coil trap on her television set that eliminated the interference the CB radio was causing and he also cleaned up the radio's frequency. He hoped that their conversations were a little more private after that.

In 1961, a few years after marriage, Paul's number was soon to come up in the draft. Paul believed that his continuing training in electronics would be more beneficial by going into the Air Force instead of the Army. He asked a good friend who worked in the recruiting office to alert him when he was about to be called up. When the call came, Paul volunteered for the Air Force before being drafted.

CHAPTER SEVEN

Military Life

After signing up for a tour of duty in the Air Force, on August 10, 1961, Paul was headed out, leaving home and his new wife for basic training in Texas.

While in basic training, during the aptitudes testing phase, Paul aced the test that is normally given at the end of the electronics training course. Therefore, he was able to bypass that training course, but would not receive the stripe normally given at course graduation time. There was a rule that you had to be in the military for a certain amount of time before you could get promoted and receive a stripe, and Paul had not been in the service long enough.

In October 1961, after basic training was over, Paul's first assignment sent him to Calumet, Michigan where Mildred was able to rejoin him, making it one of the first times she had moved a significant distance from her parents.

Paul during Basic Training

Now stationed at the Calumet Air Force Station, a radar site on the upper end of a peninsula, Paul helped to repair communication radio equipment. These radios would relay messages from airplanes flying to Alaska to the base farther south in Michigan. This was at a time during the Cold War with the threat of Russian invasion looming and before the use of satellites.

Due to Paul's knowledge of electronics surpassing the men who outranked him, they would come to him whenever they got stuck on a problem and he was able to quickly solve it. After about every 18 months of service, Paul received a promotion, along with another stripe.

Mildred and Paul in Calumet, Michigan

While in Michigan, it took most of Paul's meager paycheck for rent and gasoline, driving back and forth to the radar site on the peninsula. Mildred did not work during this time so money was very tight. They lived in a small apartment over a television repair shop and Paul would occasionally help the owner with repairs, which provided a little extra income.

Winter time in Michigan was another experience for Paul and Mildred. They were used to seeing snow while living in Missouri, but not the record breaking amount they received that winter. Most of it was lake effect snow from nearby Lake Superior, which caused a lot of snow fall with the wind making large drifts.

Upstairs apartment where Paul and Mildred lived

Because they lived in an upstairs apartment, Paul and Mildred could still see out of their windows, but the snow was up to the roof line on some houses. Driving and getting to work was always a challenge.

Around the end of May, most of the snow had melted and the ground was visible again. On Memorial Day, the town would bury all of the people that had died during the winter due to the ground being too hard and frozen to dig graves. A large ceremony would follow at the cemetery.

Mildred and Paul 1962

During the summer of 1962, the temperature only reached into the seventies. On the Fourth of July that year, Paul and Mildred wanted to go swimming in the lake like they would do back home, but it was way too cold!

Standing by a sign showing the record snowfall amount of 21.4 feet during the winter of 1950-51

New equipment was coming soon to the radar site that would upgrade them from analog to digital signals, so the Air Force sent Paul down south to Kessler Air Force Base near Biloxi, Mississippi for a ten week training course in October 1962 to learn how to service this new state-of-the-art hardware. As Paul and Mildred got close to Biloxi, he used his Citizens Band radio to ask locals if anyone knew of a house to rent for ten weeks. Thankfully, they found something right away.

Certificate from training in MS

Paul really enjoyed the training and learned all about the new digital solid-state equipment being rolled out. Two weeks after being back in Michigan and helping to get the new equipment installed, Paul received orders that he was being transferred to the country of Turkey. This confused Paul, as he never understood why they would send him to specialized training only to then send him somewhere else where that equipment was not used.

The orders of transfer came during their second winter in Michigan. Paul and Mildred left around mid-February 1963 to visit family back in Missouri before shipping out to Turkey in March to work at a radar station similar to the one in Michigan. Mildred stayed with her parents until Paul could get settled and then would send for her. Paul used about every type of transportation getting to the base. He flew into Istanbul and then rode in a taxi to the shore of the Black Sea where he caught a ferry. After crossing, he took a bus so crowded with people that he had to stand on one foot. Every bump on the road caused Paul to hit his head on the ceiling of the bus. It was only about 20 miles to the base, but it seemed like 200 as it was very uncomfortable and the smell was terrible. A few months later when Mildred came, they had to go through the whole thing again.

Paul had to personally pay $496.40 for Mildred to fly on Pan American Airways to arrive in Turkey. Even though it was an extra expense for them, Paul thought it would be a good experience for Mildred to travel, be in a foreign country, and to be with him. Paul lived in the base barracks until Mildred arrived in May and then they rented a small apartment

Paul getting ready to leave for Turkey

in the town of Yalova that had to be heated by kerosene. Before Mildred arrived, Paul had bought a cook stove which used a propane tank from another serviceman who was leaving, and also a small electric refrigerator. Both were delivered by a horse-drawn wagon via a dirt road.

Left: Apartment building - Paul and Mildred stayed on the second floor

Right: Having furniture delivered by horse drawn wagon

30

The buildings where Paul worked were close to the Black Sea and not heated, so it was usually very damp and cold. He would frequently have to wear long-johns, two pairs of pants, a sweater, and a coat to work.

In the area where they lived, it was like stepping back in time and seemed very primitive. The roads were in very poor shape. Most road work was done by hand using picks and shovels, along with a cart carrying gravel to fill potholes. It was very rare to see a tractor in the fields. Most farmers plowed their fields with horses and cows or sometimes oxen.

On the daily bus ride from Yalova to the base, Paul would pass by the Black Sea where he would see the Turkish people bathe and change clothes right on the beach. Men would just stand in the open to relieve themselves. Women had to wear burkas, clothing that covered their entire body except for their eyes. If someone tried to take a photograph of a Turkish woman, the men would confiscate their camera, but generally there was no respect for women. When Mildred would ride the bus, if there were no seats available, she was forced to stand.

In town, the bakery was a building made from rocks that contained a kiln. They made and sold a lot of bread. It was delivered by an open two-wheeled cart, down the dusty roads. The bread would get covered with dust if a car happened to drive by, but people would buy it and carry the long loaves under their hot, sweaty arms as they rode their bicycles home.

The butcher shop had no glass in the windows and no doors in the building. Dead goats and sheep just hung from the ceiling by their hind legs in the open with flies covering the meat. The store owner would just slice off part of the meat for the customer. Paul and Mildred bought their meat from the military PX, but not having a car, they had to carry their groceries home from the commissary by bus. They also bought their drinking water from the base as well. There were those who tried to sell the nicer items from the commissary to the local people, but Turkey had levied a very high fine and also a tax if anything was sold or even given away. The poor were very poor and the rich were very rich. The middle class did not exist in Turkey.

The electric generator in town would only support about 300-500 people, so electricity was only available part of each day. Paul and Mildred's refrigerator seemed to work okay on that. The water supply was a different matter. The city rationed the available water, so Paul had to pay a man to keep the barrels on their roof filled with water. From the barrels, the water ran down pipes to their water heater, which was heated with wood also purchased from the same man. Showers were taken over a hole in the floor, the sewer hole, which Americans would also place commodes over. The locals would just squat over the hole using footprints painted on the floor indicating where to stand.

Paul and Mildred in Athens, Greece

Since they did not have a lot of extra time or funds, Paul and Mildred did not get to travel much, but they did get to see a few of the areas mentioned in the Bible, such as the city of Ephesus. A Mormon group had invited them to go along with them which they did. The book of Ephesians in the Bible was written by the Apostle Paul after visiting with fellow Christians there. Another time, the Air Force chaplain on base was promoting a trip to the Holy Land. A young airman who worked with the chaplain was handling the paperwork for the trip and Paul paid him even before Mildred had arrived in Turkey. As the time for the trip approached, the airman came to Paul and wanted to give him his money back, but Paul and Mildred really wanted to go, so they refused. Later, it came out that the airman had gambled the money away, and no one that paid him got to go on the trip. He ended up in a Turkish prison and was badly treated. Paul finally did get his money back, but it took over a year.

The radio equipment at the radar station where Paul worked was constantly breaking down. He finally analyzed the problem and fixed it by changing some of the capacitors and resistors to make it a more stable circuit. The man who originally built the system flew to Turkey to find out what Paul had done to fix it and was very impressed in how much better it worked. It also helped in getting a new stripe.

In November 1963, Paul and Mildred were visiting a neighbor friend when, while listening to a new transistor radio he had just purchased, news of the assassination of President John F. Kennedy began to come over the speaker. When the man heard the news, he turned it up for everyone to hear. Everyone was shocked and in disbelief, as was much of the world.

Mildred became pregnant in 1964 with their first child while in Turkey, which Paul attributes to the very cold winter there. One day while at home in Yalova, they experienced an earthquake. This was frightening for Paul since Mildred was now pregnant. Because the old buildings were not built to handle earthquakes, they slept outside on the sidewalk for fear of violent aftershocks that might bring the building down killing them inside while they slept. After repairs had been done on the building, they moved back in and Paul ingeniously invented an earthquake alarm to alert them in the event it happened again. Seeing the lights hanging from the ceiling begin to sway during the tremors gave him the idea of wiring up two different size cans to a battery and suspending them from the ceiling, one can inside the other. If they swayed, the cans would touch each other, completing a circuit, causing the electric current to set off a buzzer. Paul and Mildred slept in their clothes and would run outside when the alarm went off.

Paul spent a total of 18 months in Turkey and Mildred about 15 months. Mildred was seven months pregnant when they finally left in November 1964, which was just under the wire according to military regulations. If they had stayed any longer, their child would have been born in Ankara, at the military hospital in Turkey's capital city. After leaving Turkey, Paul finished up his Air Force obligation at the Seymour Johnson AFB in North Carolina, working on communications equipment, radios, and transmitters. Even though he was in the Air Force, Paul always had to fly on commercial flights and never on an Air Force plane.

33

CHAPTER EIGHT

Growing the Family

While still stationed in Michigan, Paul and Mildred looked forward to having children, but were having problems conceiving. They even visited a doctor to see if anything might be preventing it, but everything looked fine. It was not until their stay in Turkey, during the long, cold winter there that they were blessed with the news that Mildred was pregnant. In November 1964, two months before their child was to be born, they were released to fly back to the States.

During a layover at the London Airport, they saw the Beatles standing at the Pan Am ticket counter preparing for a flight. It had just been eight months since the Beatles' first appearance in America on the Ed Sullivan Show. Paul and Mildred had first heard about the Beatles through newsreels shown at the Air Force base, so they immediately recognized them and Paul got a quick picture of them.

Landing in St. Louis, Paul's parents met them and took them back to Cardwell, Missouri for a two week furlough before Paul had report to the Air Force base in North Carolina. While there, family and friends threw a baby shower for Paul and Mildred's soon to arrive child. After what seemed like a too short of visit, Paul and Mildred loaded up the car and headed to North Carolina.

Visiting with Paul's parents and grandmother, Bertha Alice Statler

Once in North Carolina, they rented a house in Goldsboro and got settled in awaiting the birth of their first child. On Sunday morning, January 24th, Mildred went into labor and Paul took her to the Wayne County Memorial Hospital which was located not far from their house. Because it was the weekend, her doctor happened to be out of town and the hospital staff did not want to do anything about it. They did admit her and kept a close eye on her until the doctor arrived back to work on Monday morning. After a long, hard labor of about twenty-four hours, a bouncing baby boy was born at 5:44 a.m. on January 25, 1965. They named their new son David Paul Statler. Mildred's mother had come to help out and it was a joyous and exciting time in the Statler household.

Paul received new orders which would have sent him to the Dominican Republic and on to Vietnam shortly thereafter. Since his four-year commitment to the Air Force was complete, he decided to leave the military and return to civilian life.

In June of 1965, Paul and Mildred packed up their belongings and along with their new son, headed back to Cardwell, Missouri. Paul considered opening his repair shop again, but one had already opened while he was away in the Air Force and the small town could not support two shops. He contacted the local RCA factory outlet, where he had bought televisions that he resold in his repair shop years earlier, to inquire if anyone in the nearby area needed a repairman. Paul was immediately hired by a RCA warranty repair shop in Memphis, Tennessee to check and repair televisions along with other electronic devices. So off the family went again, moving to Memphis.

Journeyman Television Technician Completion of Apprenticeship at RCA - 1966

At about this same time, new televisions were coming out with solid-state components. Paul had a lot of knowledge with solid-state technology due to his military experiences, training, and schooling, along with all of the correspondence courses he took throughout his time in the Air Force.

During the first month at his new job, Paul was already repairing twice as many televisions as his co-worker who had worked in the shop for 17 years. His co-worker had fallen behind on the items needing fixing due to his lack of knowledge and experience compared to Paul. After a couple of months on the job, Paul's co-worker was moved out of the shop, but the Union came down hard on Paul. They wanted him to slow his production down, as he was making the others look bad, but that was not ethical to Paul. Instead, he figured out a way to increase his production by three or four times as much. Where the other repairmen fixed one item at a time, Paul used the assembly line approach. He would take ten transistor radios or televisions apart, figure out which parts needed replacing, order the parts, change out the bad parts, and get all ten items fixed at the same time. It allowed him to quickly increase the amount of work he could produce as just one person. The Union was not happy about it, but Paul could not be less productive than he knew how to be.

While working at RCA, a house-call repair ticket came in to fix one of the televisions owned by none other than Elvis Presley at his Graceland home. Paul asked if he could take the ticket and was allowed to do so. While at Graceland, he met Elvis' grandmother and his father, but Elvis was not home at the time. Elvis' father even gave Paul a tour of the house after fixing the television. Paul kept the part that went bad, a small resistor, as a memento of his visit. He went back to Graceland two more times, once to fix a stereo and another time to fix a television in Elvis' bedroom. Elvis had three televisions total in the bedroom so that no matter which way he laid in bed, he could watch a screen. Many years later, Paul watched a television special celebrating the 75th birthday of Elvis. During the program, one of the rooms from Graceland was shown and it was the same room where Paul had fixed that first television. The room looked exactly the same as when he was there so many years before.

Mildred's father Millard passed away on May 14, 1967. A few years earlier, he had developed lung cancer due to a lifetime of smoking. It got to the point where he could not run the farm in Cardwell any longer, so he sold all of their equipment and bought a house in Paragould, Arkansas in 1966. He came and stayed with Paul and Mildred in Memphis when he traveled to the hospital there for treatments. He also gained a renewed interest in attending church about this time. After his passing, Mildred's mother Arlene, a self-taught seamstress, began doing clothing alterations at a store in downtown Paragould and worked there for many years.

Jewel, Arlene, Millard, and Mildred - 1962

After working for RCA two years, the company offered Paul a branch manager position. Around this same time, the Veteran's Administration was about to open a new hospital there in Memphis and had an opening for an electronics technician. Paul was hired by the VA in July of 1967. On his first day, he saw a man die. The patient was just released and on his way home when he became sick, so his wife turned the car around and headed back to the hospital. After arriving, the hospital staff performed CPR on him, but he passed away. This event really bothered Paul and made a lasting impression. Right then he made the decision to be a part of helping keep people alive and well.

Paul's initial duties at the hospital were supporting the communications systems. This included everything from the two-way radios between staff, call systems to nurses' stations, televisions in patients' rooms, to the vacuum tube system that carried messages and medications all across the hospital. During the construction of a new VA hospital in town, he reworked the electronics that programmed the tube system to improve the service it gave delivering medicines from the pharmacy to the nurses' stations and ran miles of wire for the installation of the paging system.

One Christmas during this time, Paul and Mildred bought a slot-car race track set for their son David, which took up most of the living room floor. David was very excited, obviously, but did not get to play with it much that Christmas day. A young pastor was invited over for lunch, and after eating, the pastor and Paul began playing with the cars, racing them around the track. Paul remembers hearing his young son say, "I want to play," and feels real bad for leaving him out.

Close to a year after starting at the VA, Paul was moved into supporting the medical equipment side due to the help he provided to the supervisor in that area. The supervisor was servicing one of the ultrasound machines and after pushing the safety switch, a diode shorted out and caused a capacitor to blow up. Paul told him that he would work on the machine and was able to fix the problem. After fixing a few other issues for him, the supervisor got Paul transferred over to the medical side of technology services.

Not long after Paul made the move to medical equipment support, the hospital performed its first open-heart surgery. As the on-duty medical technician, Paul was right there in the operating room during this first surgery monitoring the heart rate and blood pressure equipment. If something should go wrong with the equipment, Paul was responsible for getting it replaced immediately. Another piece of equipment he monitored was the artificial heart pump.

David Statler circa 1968

Paul admits that seeing his own blood will cause him to become light-headed or even faint. Even though witnessing that first open-heart surgery was pretty gory to watch, he never once fainted as he knew that what he was doing was a very important part of the surgery by keeping the equipment going.

Part of Paul's daily duties included checking the various types of equipment in the Intensive Care Unit (ICU). Since this took up a lot time each day, he designed a piece of equipment for more accurate and faster testing, for which he received an award from the hospital. Medical equipment had to be closely monitored to make sure it was functioning correctly.

In the ICU, electrodes are attached to a patient's chest to monitor the electrocardiogram (EKG) readings. Problems would occur when the saline gel on the electrode patches would dry out requiring the nurses to change out all of them, even the ones that had not dried out yet, so the monitoring would start up again. This was very uncomfortable for the patient each time the nurses had to pull off the patches from their skin. Seeing the problem, Paul found a solution by building and inserting a small tester into the cable that monitored the moisture level of each patch. Now the nurses only had to swap out the ones that were actually dry. This was a lot more comfortable for the patient and it saved the nurses time.

An upper-level co-worker encouraged Paul to obtain a Bachelor's degree. Deciding that this was a good direction for advancement, he began taking night classes at a local college. Attending a technical institute to take an electronics course of study, he along with three other guys, were required to take an entry-level course before they were allowed to take the more advanced courses. Because of their prior experience, all four of them were well versed in the basic understanding of electronics. Soon after classes started, it became very apparent to the four of them that the teacher did not have a clue what he was trying to teach. Knowing something was wrong, they all went to visit the Dean of the school and requested to see the teacher's credentials. The Dean admitted that they were still waiting on them since this teacher was newly hired. The Dean then demanded from the teacher his credentials and discovered he was certified to teach in music, not electronics. He was immediately fired and replaced by a more suitable instructor.

Mildred and David
Easter 1968

The garage for the house where Paul and Mildred lived was a separate building from the house. Paul rigged up a remote start device for the car to get it warmed up during the winter. Inside the garage, he had a small workbench setup for doing repairs on radios and televisions. A friend brought over a radio for Paul to repair and while working on it, he told the friend that he had to go to the house to retrieve something. Leaving the friend in the garage, Paul entered the house and pressed the switch to remote start the car, which also raised the garage door. After shutting the car off, Paul returned to the garage only to find his friend walking down the driveway. Asking where he was going, the friend who was clearly spooked replied, "You aren't going to believe this, but the garage door went up and your car started all by itself!" Paul had a hard

David's fourth birthday
January 1969

time getting the friend to come back into the garage, but after he told him what had really happened, they had a good laugh.

Paul was also instrumental in starting a choir in the VA hospital chapel. One morning Paul and a coworker heard the organ playing in the chapel and upon entering they began singing the hymn the organist was playing. She said, "You guys sound pretty good. Do you want to come again?" They did and after inviting a few more people, it was not long before they had roughly 25 in attendance, rehearsing each morning at 7:40 a.m., before work. They called their choir the "Seven Forty Airs" and even the main office in Washington wanted their picture noting them as "the only volunteer employee choir in the VA." During Easter that year, a record number of 144 people attended the hospital chapel services.

During the summer of 1969, Paul and Mildred bought a push-pedal fire truck for their son David. It had a little bell that rang by pulling an attached string and David pedaled it all around their backyard. Paul later added an old lawn mower engine to it and hooked up a speaker on the hood that would blare out a loud siren sound. Donning his red fireman's hat, David could now get to the fire in style.

This was also the summer of the first moon landing (July 20, 1969). Paul had three television sets hooked up in the family room to be able to watch all three networks' coverage of the moon landing. Paul hooked up a headset so that one television's audio was in the left ear and another television's audio was in the right ear. The third television's audio just came through its speakers.

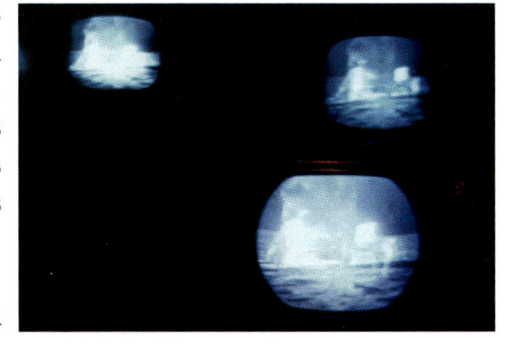

In 1969, Mildred became pregnant with their second child. As it approached Labor Day weekend, Mildred's doctor assured her that the delivery was still a few days away. Therefore, Paul and Mildred decided it would be safe to attend a Labor Day picnic. Mildred started having labor pains earlier than expected, so both she and Paul hurriedly made arrangements for their son David to spend the night at their next door neighbor's house and then headed to the Methodist Hospital. Their beautiful new baby girl Mary Elizabeth Statler was born on September 3, 1969 at 2:54 a.m.

Mary Elizabeth Statler

While Mildred stayed in the hospital for a few days, Paul ventured into unknown territory by trying to cook for his young son and himself. David remembers waiting patiently at the kitchen table while Paul tried cooking hotdogs in a pot full of boiling water on the stove.

In 1971, while Paul was gaining a lot of experience working on medical equipment, two related positions within the VA system became available. One was located in Lexington, Kentucky, and the other in Columbia, Missouri. Paul was told, "If you want to be promoted, this is an excellent opportunity." Paul and Mildred did not think twice about wanting to move back to Missouri. Paul's parents were living in Advance, Missouri at the time and his sister lived in the St. Louis area. Mildred's brother lived in Kansas and her mother in Arkansas, so Columbia seemed like an ideal spot to travel from to all of these locations. It also seemed like a good time to move away from Memphis. Paul's son David had just finished kindergarten and there was still unrest in the city due to the assassination of Martin Luther King, Jr. even though it had been three years past.

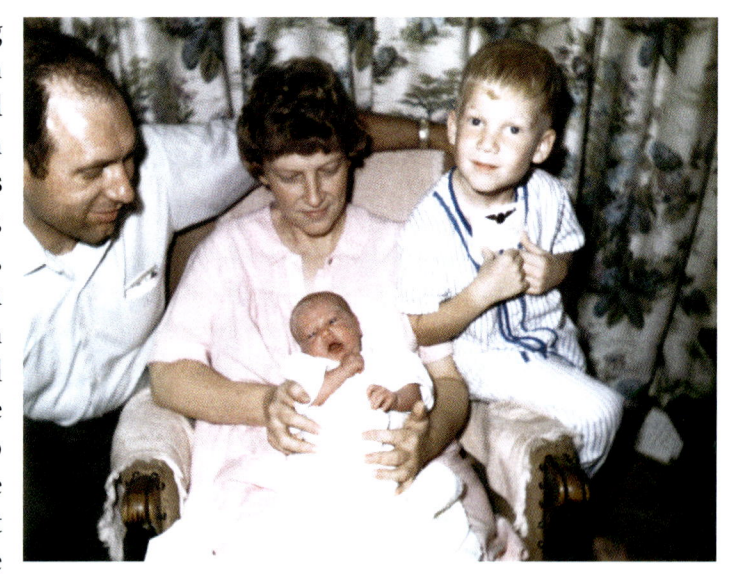

The position of Supervisor of Medical Equipment required a Bachelor's degree, but Paul made the decision to apply anyway. The position would be at the brand new Harry S Truman VA hospital in Columbia which was to open within the next year. Paul hopped in his Chevrolet Caprice and headed northwest. Before arriving, he experienced car problems, but was able to repair them, made it to the interview which went very well, and they hired him on the spot. Excitedly, he went looking for a house and found one in the Valley View subdivision on Lilac Drive in the north part of Columbia, but would not be able to move in until two weeks later.

Mary Statler - Age 2
Columbia, Missouri - September 1971

The family stayed in a Columbia hotel until they could move into their new home. Since it was summertime, they spent most evenings in the hotel's pool. On one particular evening, Paul was trying to teach his six year old son how to swim. He was holding David underneath his body allowing him to kick his feet and move his arms. During this "lesson," Paul looked over and saw his young two year old daughter Mary going down under the water, her long blonde hair floating up to the surface. Knowing she could not swim, Paul instinctively dropped David and rushed over to pull Mary up out of the water. She had held her breath and came up laughing, but David had panicked over the shock of being dropped and going underwater and came up screaming. Paul yelled to him to just put his feet down since he was not in too deep of water.

One disappointment for Paul was that he was unable to complete his Bachelor's degree since the courses he needed to finish were not offered in the evening by the local colleges. Paul did take a variety of other night courses at an adult career center to further his knowledge in electronics, computers, welding, air conditioning, and even physiology (as to understand medical terminology better). He also took classes on sales and completed the Dale Carnegie course. He was voted runner-up to the one who advanced the most since the start of the class.

David playing out in the snow
Columbia, Missouri - 1971

CHAPTER NINE

VA in Columbia

Paul's experiences working on X-ray machines, operating room and ICU equipment at the Memphis VA came in very handy at his new job in Columbia. He worked very closely with the purchasing agent for the new hospital and oversaw the installation of the new X-ray machines and various other pieces of equipment. The new hospital finally opened with the first patient admitted on April 4, 1972. The hospital continues to serve veterans to this day. Paul was right there in the operating room, always monitoring the equipment. After about twenty-five open heart surgeries, he began to train others on his staff to do what he was doing. It was a very interesting first few years for Paul in his new supervisory role, learning about new technologies, dealing with vendors, and hiring people who could repair and monitor the equipment.

Paul believed in hiring people that had the right qualifications, looked respectable, and had good character. One time a man came to his interview in a suit and tie, looked nice and was well qualified for the job. On his first day of the job, he came to work dressed in jeans with holes in them and was half drunk. This created a bad start right way. Turned out he had a drinking problem, poor hygiene, and used bad language. The man did not last very long on the job.

Paul Statler outside of the Veterans Hospital in Columbia, MO

Paul worked a normal 40 hour week like most employees there, but as a supervisor, he was also on-call anytime there was an emergency. He oversaw the maintenance, safety, upkeep, and the upgrading of all the medical equipment in the hospital. Paul really enjoyed the work and saw the vital and important part it played in the workings of a hospital.

In view of the safety aspect alone, just attaching monitoring electrodes to a patient could result in harm or even electrocution if safety protocols were not followed. Paul trained all of the nurses on electrical safety and the equipment was constantly tested to make sure it stayed in good working order as well.

Vendors selling the latest models of medical equipment approached Paul all the time. He would compare the technologies of the equipment as well as the brands. It was not his job to deal with the financial aspect of the items, but to make sure the equipment did what it said it would do and make recommendations regarding the choices. Paul was interested in finding the best equipment to do the job, before it was ever hooked up to a patient.

CHAPTER TEN

The Move to Englewood

During his first year at the VA, Paul and a friend decided to each buy some acreage about 20 miles south of Columbia, in the small community of Englewood, Missouri. They each bought three and one-half acres of adjoining property to build their houses on and to enjoy some garden space. After getting the basements dug, Paul's friend was transferred elsewhere and therefore sold his land to Paul now giving the family a full seven acres. Once the house was built and enclosed, Paul did a lot of the inside work himself, using his weekends to install the wiring, plumbing, woodworking, painting, and all the finishing touches. It also gave Paul space to put up the Martin bird house his father had made him years before. Since Paul and Mildred both grew up on farms, they thought the farming community and living on a farm would be important for the kids.

It was not the typical farm, as there was no barn built on the land and the family did not raise any farm-type animals like chickens or cows. They did cultivate part of the land to set up and plant two large gardens. Paul and Mildred tried their hands at growing a variety of items: okra, corn, squash, green beans, strawberries, cucumbers, pumpkins, cantaloupe, and even peanuts. Once they grew a 60 pound pumpkin in the patch. Mildred canned a lot of the items they grew as well. One year she canned 150 quarts of green beans!

Mildred picking okra

One year Paul tried growing mush-melons. When he thought they should be ripe, he would cut one open, but it was still green inside. After doing this

44

for a while, Paul was confused why the melons were not ripening. After mentioning this to a coworker, he told Paul that some melons always stay green on the inside, even after ripening. By this time, most of the melons were past the ripened stage and had begun to rot.

Now that they were out in the country, the kids were able to have pets. David selected a dog and Mary picked out a cat. Paul also got a Shetland pony for the kids, but it was very contrary and ornery which caused a lot of headaches. If he did not want you to ride him, he would just lay down. A neighbor said to just tie his feet together when he did that and let him lay there for awhile. Paul did and the pony never attempted to lie down again after that. One day while Mary was riding, the pony got spooked by the lawn mower and Mary fell off. The pony's hoof was on her chest, but he knew somehow not to hurt her. Paul was still scared by the event and eventually gave the pony away.

Skipper the Shetland pony

With the pony gone, the thrill of riding was replaced by a small blue mini-bike. Before David was allowed to ride it, Paul instructed him on all of the customary safety precautions and proper use of the bike's brakes and throttle. When it was time for David to take his first test ride, he gave it full throttle and took off at top speed. Going down a small hill by the house, he wiped out, thankfully unhurt, but learned an important life lesson: Do what your father tells you and pay attention!

Mary on the mini-bike

A year or so later, Paul bought a slightly larger bike, a Honda 50cc. The gravel road in front of the house was a five mile loop which made it convenient to take rides from the house and back again. Once, Paul was taking his daughter Mary for a ride on the original mini-bike and David was out in front riding the Honda. At the farthest point in the loop, the mini-bike stopped running and Paul starting yelling at David to stop. Unable to hear his father over the sound of his bike, David just continued on home, never looking back. Once home, Mildred asked him, "Where are Dad and Mary?" Mildred got in the car and went looking for them. She found Paul walking and carrying Mary.

Paul had also bought a go-kart that Mary rode all over the seven acres. On the "back-forty," they would let the grass grow real tall, then brush-hog paths to drive it through.

Mary driving the go-kart

The house was built with a full basement which Paul finished out with a couple of bedrooms, bathroom, full kitchen, laundry area, and a large family room. The kitchen is where Mildred did the canning of items picked from their garden. In the family room was a ping-pong table, which was one sport Paul loved playing with family and friends. He started David off as soon as he was tall enough to reach the top of the table, running him back and forth from corner to corner.

It was around this time, in 1977, that Mildred's mother remarried. She married Luther Cline, an old friend who had lost his wife in a car accident just the year before. He was a very kind and gentle man who loved and cared for Arlene. They continued to live in Arlene's house in Paragould until his death in 2001.

Some of Paul's neighbors and friends wanted to start a small community church and began meeting in Paul's basement family room each week. As the church began to grow, it was decided by the group to hire a pastor, but the church did not have enough money to also pay for a parsonage. Paul and Mildred volunteered their newly remodeled basement to the young family of four to temporarily stay for a few weeks until they could find a more permanent home. Those few weeks turned into six months and Paul arrived home from work one day to find the pastor and his wife putting up their own mailbox next to his. It was at this time that Paul asked them to move out. The small church continued to meet at a different location and is still active even today.

Arlene and Luther Cline

Paul was also active in the small community by helping to teach a group of young boys in the local Englewood 4-H group about electricity. He instructed them on how to build small projects to help them learn the elements of electricity and some of them entered their projects in the Boone County fair. Years later, a grandfather came up to Paul to thank him for working with his grandson. When the grandson had graduated high school, he got a job working with a company that builds electronics and has been very successful with that company for many years. Paul's son David credits his father for helping him with his school's science fair projects as well. One such project allowed testing of how much resistance the body has. Holding onto two small prongs enabled the body to complete the electrical circuit and a small circle of lights would light up.

On January 28, 1978, Paul was informed that his father Coy had passed away. Paul, now nearly 40 years old, remembers this

Mildred and Coy Statler
40th Wedding Anniversary
October 9, 1975
Van Buren, Missouri

46

being very painful, both losing his father and having to tell his son David who had just turned thirteen three days earlier. Paul does not remember much about the funeral; it was just too sad for him. Coy was laid to rest in the Cape County Memorial Park Cemetery in Cape Girardeau, Missouri. Paul states that his life story might have been very different without the attention of his father. Paul's parents were living in Van Buren, Missouri at the time of his father's death. Paul's mother, being a licensed minister herself, was the pastor of the Methodist church there until her retirement in early 1982. In November of 1982, she remarried to Jeff Sellers.

Paul, Mildred, his mother Mildred, nephew Wesley Blaylock, and daughter Mary outside of the Van Buren Methodist Church

The Statlers lived in Englewood for six years. With economic times getting tougher in the late seventies, Paul and Mildred began thinking seriously about moving back closer to Columbia. Almost every day they drove back and forth to Columbia for work, shopping, and church, putting 50 miles or more on the car each time. In 1977-78, gasoline was rationed and continually increasing in cost. With the prediction that heating prices would double in the next year and with the house being all electric, Paul began researching the idea of building a more energy efficient solar home. When Paul announced the forthcoming move to his children, their son David was heartbroken. He was thirteen that summer, between his seventh and eighth grades in school. He did not want to leave all the friends he had made in school and in the community. He even taped a handwritten "NOT" to the For Sale sign in the front yard. Eventually the house did sell and the family moved into a duplex while their new home was being built just south of Columbia.

CHAPTER ELEVEN

Back in Columbia

Being in new surroundings was not easy at first for David. Coming home from the first day at his new school, he missed the drop-off point where he was supposed to get off the bus. As the only kid left on the bus, he told the bus driver who graciously delivered him back to his stop.

It was while living in the duplex that Paul bought his first computer, a Radio Shack TRS-80. He and David were excited about learning how to run programs (which were loaded via cassette tapes) and more about this new technology. Not long after having the computer, a friend of Paul's offered to trade an Apple II computer for the TRS-80 which Paul agreed to do. The serial number on the Apple computer was #525. A year or so later, this same friend opened an Apple store in town and offered to trade Paul a brand new Apple II Plus computer for the older Apple II. Paul took him up on the offer to take advantage of the newer technology.

Vintage Apple II Computer

Mildred, Paul, Bob, and Shirley Olson Getting baptised in the Jordan River during their trip to Israel in 2005

Bob Olson and his wife Shirley have been close friends with Paul and Mildred since 1972 and have attended church together as well. Bob was the Laundry Supervisor at the VA hospital and using the Apple computer, he and Paul designed and wrote a computer program to track various statistics on laundry usage and costs. Bob and Paul both received awards for their work on the program as well. When the Main Office saw the cost savings going on, they wanted to take Paul's computer, but he told them they would have to get their own since it was his own personal device. Soon after that, the hospital bought a mainframe which Paul helped to train a lot of people on.

48

In the summer of 1979, Paul took his family on an extended two-week vacation out West. They visited a lot of the major sites: Grand Canyon National Park, Old Faithful at Yellowstone National Park, Devil's Tower National Monument, Petrified Forest National Park, Badlands National Park, Four Corners Monument, Mount Rushmore National Memorial Park, Pike's Peak, the Mormon Tabernacle, The Great Salt Lake, Reptile Gardens, Royal Gorge Bridge, and the Dam Store. The family traveled in a pick-up truck with a camper shell over the bed, pulling a pop-up camper. They stayed at camping sites and never had to stay in a hotel. This particular vacation holds many memories for the family.

The Statler family atop Mt. Evans

The family also did a lot of weekend camping during the summertime. They had makeshift beds in the back of the pickup with the camper shell and would camp by the Missouri River and other campgrounds around Missouri, along with exploring caves or canoeing on various rivers.

Mary riding a tortoise at Reptile Gardens in South Dakota

Technological changes were happening all the time at the VA. There was never a dull moment and Paul admits to loving the challenge. He also helped in the laboratory for medical students, which was part of the VA. Paul was once helping some doctors with the development of "seeing" the sound of the ultrasound machine by using a computer. One night, Paul was awakened at 2 a.m. with one of the doctors he had been working with heavily on his mind. The impression of this doctor, also named Paul, was so strong that Paul decided to call his office and was surprised that he answered the phone. Paul, sensing frustration in the doctor's voice, asked him, "Are you okay?"

He responded, "I'm trying to figure out this one circuit, the one to convert the audio to video. I've been praying that an answer would come." Soon after that prayer was uttered is when Paul called his office. After discussing the issue for awhile, Paul happened to know how to overcome the problem and the doctor was able to make the conversion, helping him in the further development of ultrasound technology.

CHAPTER TWELVE

The Solar Home

In addition to the rising costs of living in Englewood, the rural setting just was not the same as when Paul and Mildred had grown up. Life was now very different. After moving back to Columbia, they purchased a tract of land, which was three miles from their church and two and a half miles to school. The year before, Paul had begun taking some evening classes at the University of Missouri on solar energy and building those efficiencies into a home. Later an architect was hired to put Paul's vision on paper and a contractor was hired to begin the building process.

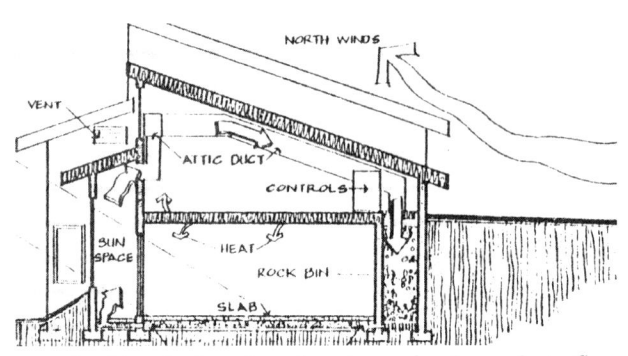

Architect's drawing showing solar heated air flow

The house was to be built into the slope of a hill. They dug back into the hill 10 feet and put in a concrete wall 10 feet high and 80 feet wide which was later extended. Gravel, along with drain pipes to avoid ground moisture seepage, was installed in the ground. On top of that was laid special dense 2-inch foam insulation. On the insulation was placed 2-feet of 4-inch sized rock for air flow. Finally on top of that was built the regular framework of flooring.

Four feet in front of the north side wall, a second 10-foot high concrete wall was put up. The space in between the walls was filled with more of the 4-inch rock. Concrete blocks, turned sideways, allowed air flow through the rock in the wall down to the rock under the floor.

Once the house was framed in and the outside walls enclosed, the family moved out of the duplex and lived in the pop-up camper which was set up inside the garage of the new home. This was more convenient for Paul

Paul standing over the space that will hold the rock used for storing heat

to work on the inside of the house in the evenings and saved money by not having to pay rent on the duplex.

The house, once completed, was three stories tall and brought in heat several ways. On the entire south side of the house was the sun-room, or "greenhouse," which the sun would heat during the day. All the rooms attached to the sun-room had sliding glass doors to allow heat and light into the rooms. The warm air in the sun-room, which could reach 100-degrees at the top of the third floor, was blown via a fan through air vents into the rock stored in the walls and floor which would store the heat. The air coming out of the vents after moving through the rock would come out at a very comfortable temperature.

Paul inspecting the building progress

It would not be until a few weeks into February that more energy was needed for heating than what was stored in the rocks. A small wood stove was used to supplement and back-up electric baseboard heaters were also installed in the rooms, but were rarely used.

Windows are the cause of most heat loss in a home. With a home having the entire south side made of windows, there was a lot of heat loss at night when it was cold and dark. After seeing a demonstration of a bead-wall system, Paul decided to install a similar system to insulate the house at night to avoid heat loss. The south side windows in the sun-room were double-paned, with about 5-inches between the panes. At night, tiny Styrofoam beads were blown in between the panes to create an insulating barrier. Also, because they were white in color, they reflected the lights that were turned on inside the house which increased the brightness in the adjacent rooms.

In the morning, the tiny beads were pumped back out of the windows and stored in big storage tanks made of 55 gallon drums, welded on top of each other, stacked three high. Vacuum cleaner motors were used to move the beads from the drums to the windows and back again. Switches were used in the beginning to turn it on and off, but Paul later computerized it with light sensors so that when the sun went down, the beads would automatically move into the windows and back out with the morning light.

This method was not without its issues. Static electricity buildup was one problem Paul had to overcome by occasionally treating the foam beads with glycerin. Although this solved the issue of beads sticking to the windows, the glycerin would leave a coating that Paul had to clean. A dirt dauber's nest once clogged a passageway for the beads. Thinking it was due to not enough power from the motors, Paul installed a larger motor. Since that did not help, he then knew that there was a clog somewhere along the path. After determining where the clog was and removing the nest, it ran fine after that. Another time a connection in one of the pipes carrying the beads separated blowing beads all over the place. Paul was very proud of this insulating system and showed it off whenever people visited. One year, the house was a stop on a tour of solar homes in the area and the bead-wall system was the highlight of the tour.

Because Paul knew that Styrofoam is dangerous when it burns, the particular beads he purchased came with fire retardant on them. Later, speaking to the local fire department, they warned him that Styrofoam could give off poisonous fumes. Furthermore, the storage drums were taking up a lot of space in the attic. Even though it had helped in insulating, because of these and other issues, and deciding that it was just not practical overall, Paul removed the bead-wall system.

The sun heated everything, including their hot water. Paul purchased a 1,500-gallon hot water tank from a university auction. After resealing, re-piping, and painting it, he also built a heat exchanger for it. There were solar collectors on the roof of the house that heated the water. Before using the new solar water heating system, the family was constantly running out of hot water, especially with two children taking long showers. They never ran out of hot water again after installing the new tank.

Paul used a second heat exchanger made of flexible copper pipe wrapped in a coil around their wood stove. This heated water would circulate to the water heater and minimize the amount of electricity needed to heat the water.

Mildred a few years after building completion

During the construction of the home, Paul did all of the electrical wiring himself and made it completely convenient for turning lights on and off. You could walk all the way through the house without having to go back to turn off a light. Even with light switches controlling the lights from both entrances and exits in every room, Paul still found lights left on in the house. He finally determined it was the kids. He got the "bright" idea to correct this bad habit by giving each child a dollar's worth of nickels. A child would have to pay a nickel for every light left on. The child with the most nickels at the end of the week would be paid $10. If Paul left a light on, he had to pay them a nickel.

A few years later, the house went through some big changes. A friend who did research at the VA hospital asked Paul, "What are you doing about radon gas?" Paul had never heard of this, but later learned that radon gas naturally seeps up from rocky soil. There was a lot of rock under and round the house, so Paul purchased some radon gas testing devices and positioned them in the bedrooms, kitchen, and in the rock storage area. The results came back at a Level 4, which is not very high, but suggested something be done about it. Due to breathing re-circulated air inside the envelope of the house, this level of radon gas in the air was equivalent to smoking one cigarette a day. Knowing that this was not healthy in the long term, Paul made the decision to remove the rock between the two 10-foot walls and turn the space into storage.

Over the years the house went through many changes, but Paul and Mildred continue benefiting from much of what was initially built.

House with added garage/workshop at the far end

Paul and his cousin Pansy (left)   *Paul and his mother Mildred*   *Mildred and her brother Jewel*

Paul with his sister, parents, and grandmother Bertha Alice Statler

Paul and his parents   *Paul and Mildred with their parents*   *Wedding Reception*

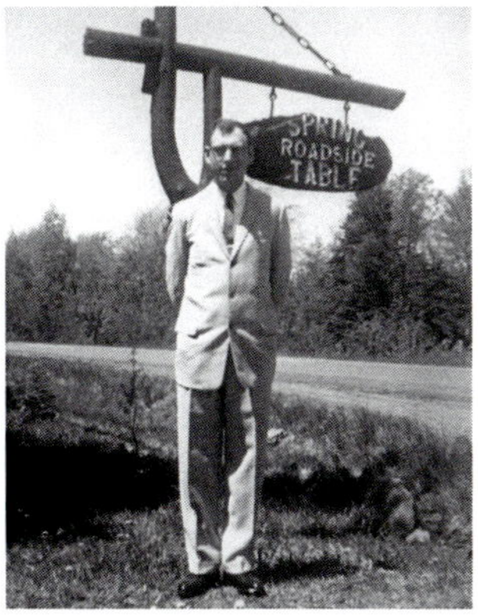
SPRING
ROADSIDE
TABLE
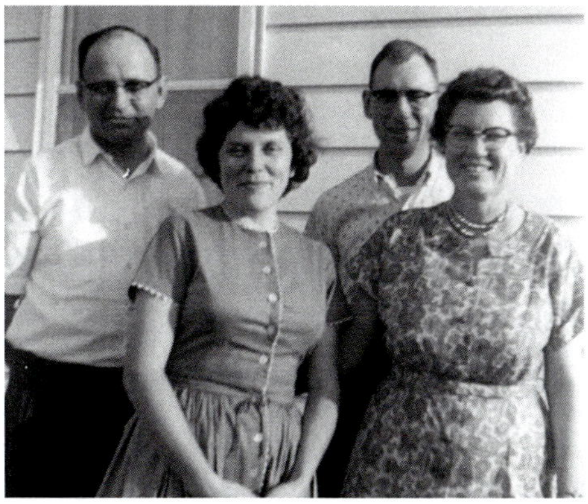
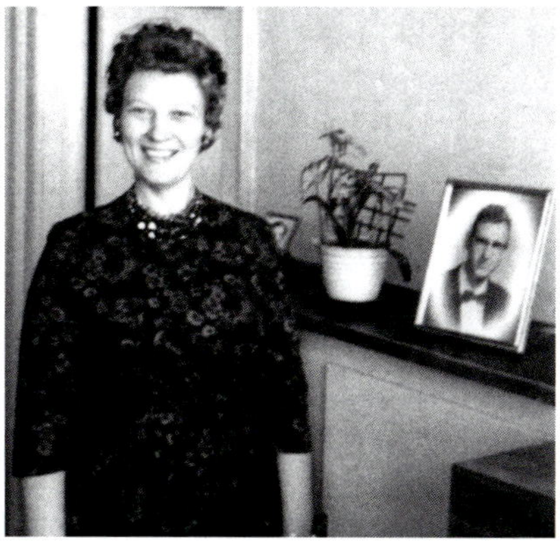
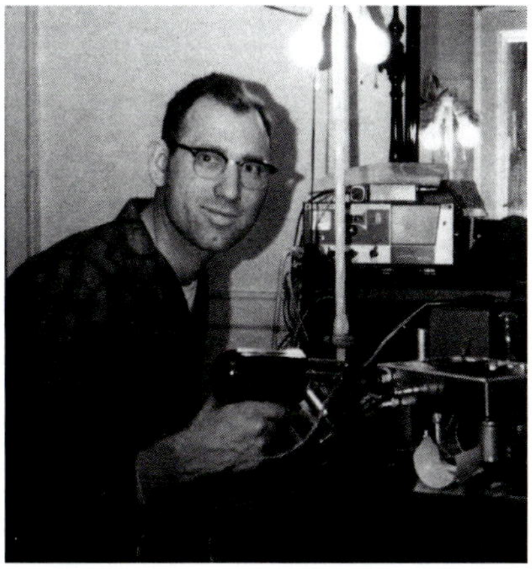
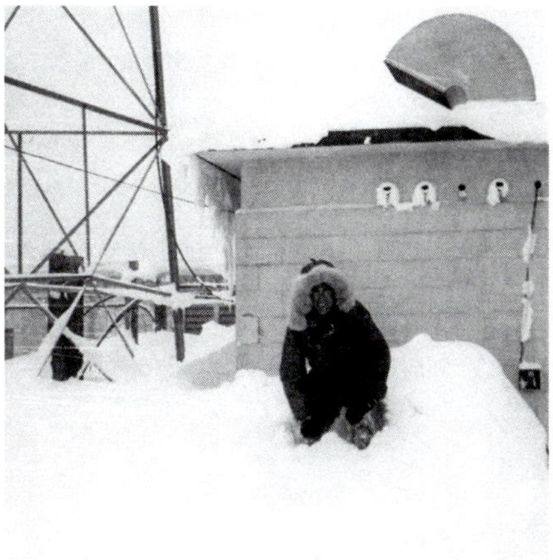
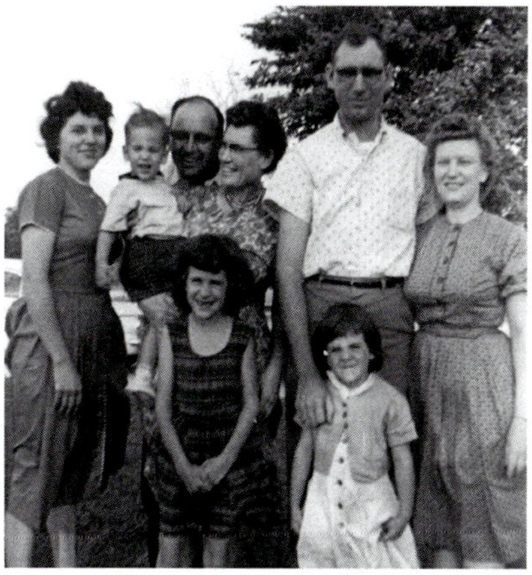
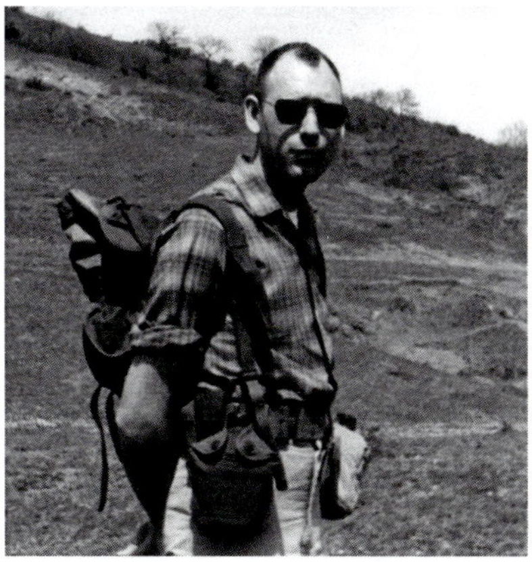
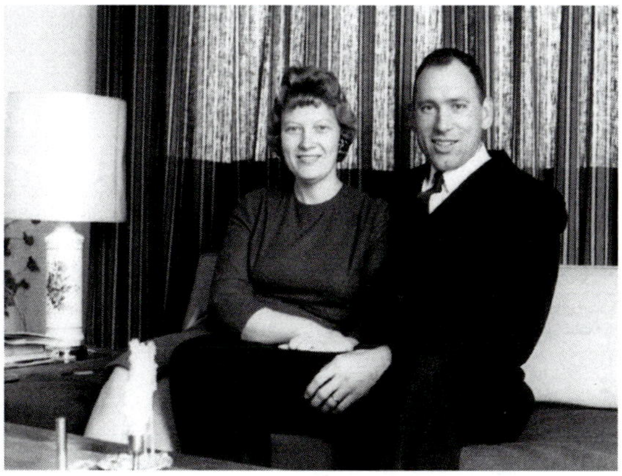
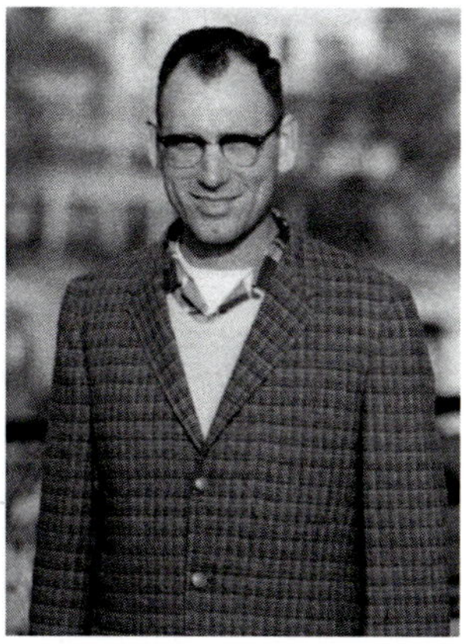
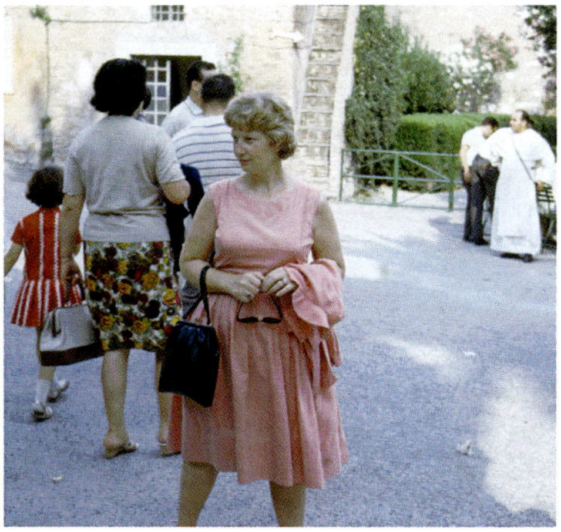
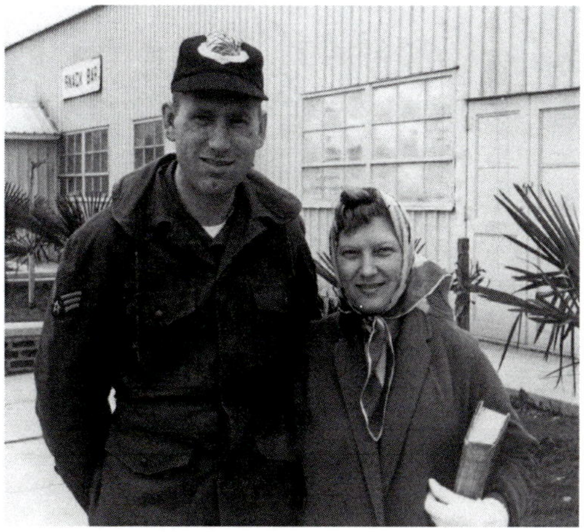

Paul with son David

David and Mary Elizabeth

That 70's Family

40th Wedding Anniversary

Paul and Mildred helped develop soccer fields

Paul working on one of his many projects

Mildred in New York

Paul and Mildred on their Alaskan cruise

Mildred in London

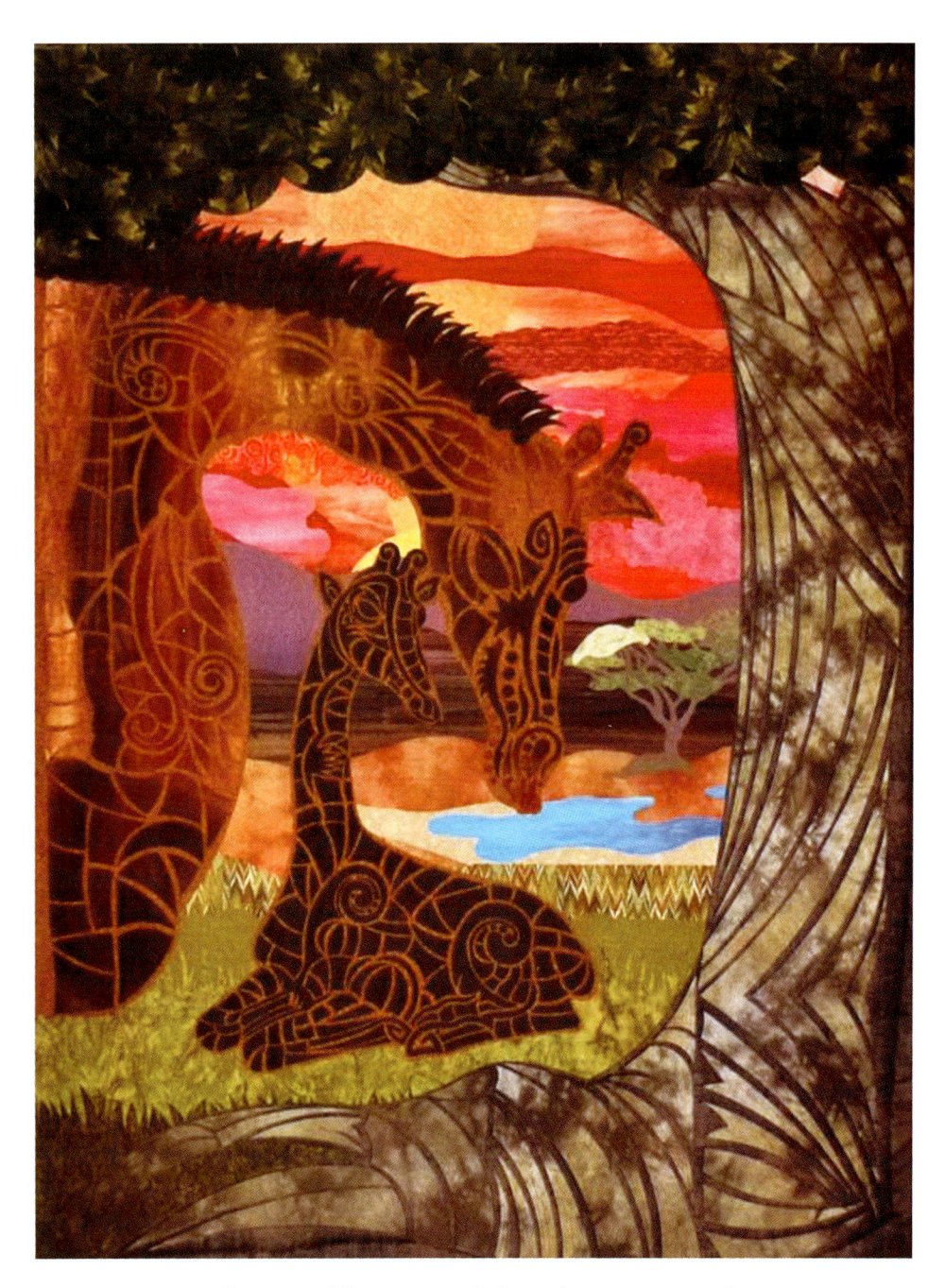

"Serengeti" by Jo Ann Blade and Kim Diamond

PART TWO

STATLER
THE MACHINE

CHAPTER THIRTEEN

A Dream Come True

Paul had taken his family to the Missouri State Fair in Sedalia many times over the years to observe the display of agricultural, mechanical, and natural resource offerings from around the State. Mildred liked viewing the many baking, sewing, and quilting entries, particularly the blue-ribbon winning displays. Paul enjoyed watching the truck and tractor pull events and the children loved riding the midway rides.

While attending the fair in 1988, Paul and Mildred spotted, for the first time, a vendor showing off a longarm quilting machine. They watched as a lady demonstrated how she could sew patterns on a quilt by guiding the head of the machine by hand and following the pattern printed on paper with a pointer. Upon seeing this in action, Paul's first thought was, "That should be automated!"

Already being familiar with CNC (computer numerical control) equipment, which is used to create motion controls via computers, Paul mentioned to Mildred, "I want to put a computer on that machine. Wouldn't you like that, Mildred?" "Not really. I don't want to work that hard," she replied. After leaving the fair, Paul did not think about it much as other projects and activities took up his time.

Tim and Mary (Statler) Foley
November 1988

Later that year in November, Paul and Mildred's daughter Mary was married to Tim Foley, the son of long-time family friends Leon and Norma Foley.

During Christmas, Paul and his family traveled to Florida to visit his mother Mildred. She was struggling with colon cancer and the visit lifted her spirits. Just a few months later in February of 1989, Paul's sister Mary Alice and her family also traveled to Florida to visit their mother. Mary Alice called Paul and stated, "if you want to see your mother alive one more time, you'd better come now." Paul quickly made arrangements and flew down to Florida. Their mother's health had gone downhill very quickly since he had seen her at Christmas. After consulting with a doctor, it was determined that she needed a blood transfusion. True to her ministry of witnessing to those around her about Jesus, she spoke about His love to the attendants in the ambulance on the way to the hospital. The next day, Paul's mother

Paul's mother Mildred and sister Mary Alice December 1986

was allowed to return home. Sitting by her bedside, Paul earnestly prayed for a healing miracle in his mother's life. Throughout her ministry, she had prayed for many people who received God's touch and were healed. Even as he held her hand and prayed, she slipped from this life into eternity. For quite some time after this, Paul struggled with his faith. He questioned why God would not spare someone who did so much for Him, but others who never professed to be a follower of Christ continued to prosper. He was still a deacon at church during this time, but dealing with a shaken faith, Paul had a hard time praying for those that came to him for prayer during church services. Eventually, he knew that God did heal his mother by releasing her from her broken body and taking her to her heavenly home. This knowledge brought much peace to Paul.

Three months later in May of 1989, their son David was married to Tricia Hales. She was from northwest Missouri and moved to Columbia to attend the University of Missouri. David and Tricia met through a campus ministry and attended Christian Chapel together with his family.

Paul had also volunteered his time over the last eight years serving on the Active Electronics Advisory Committee, which gave insight and direction to the Columbia Area Vocational Technical School's electronics program. At the end of the current school year, Paul decided to resign his activities on the committee and on May 23, 1989, the school presented him with a "Certificate of Honor" for his dedication and guidance to the school.

Wedding of Paul and Mildred's son David to Tricia Hales - May 1989

In the fall of 1989, Paul and Mildred attended the State Fair and once again saw the long-arm quilting machine. This time, the man who owned the machine was giving demonstrations in the booth. After Paul introduced himself, he told the owner of his plans that he would like to buy a machine and automate the process. Thomas "Tom" (not his real name) told Paul that he had been looking for someone to do just that and invited him to visit his factory.

Tom's factory was an hour and a half drive away from Columbia, located in a small town where Paul had never been. Arriving in town, Paul rounded a corner and saw the factory building. Paul thought to himself that he had been here before, but that could not be because he knew he had never visited here before. However, the surroundings looked so familiar. A feeling of déjà vu hit Paul as he parked and got out of the car. Then it became clear to him. Everything was exactly as it was in his recurring dream. Now it was staring him in the face, 33 years later.

When he initially began having this dream, Paul did not pay much attention to it, but after having the same dream about this factory several times, he began to take careful note of the details. It was always a factory setting with two buildings connected by an enclosed walkway which had a large 12-inch chuckhole in the middle of the concrete. In the dream, he would enter one of the factory buildings and see many familiar pieces of equipment, but there was always one piece of equipment that Paul did not recognize.

That fateful day in 1989, standing there outside of his car, there was his dream in real life. There were the two buildings exactly as he saw in his dream. As Paul walked into the main shop building, he saw tables of equipment identical to what he remembered. He could have closed his eyes and walked through Tom's factory. Going through the walkway between buildings, there was the hole in the concrete floor the same as in the dream. Upon entering the second building, he saw his first aluminum welder, with the special head just as he had dreamed about.

Through the fulfillment of this dream, Paul knew in his heart that God was leading him to proceed with this endeavor. He made arrangements for Tom to deliver a quilting machine head and wood table on loan to his house that he could begin working on to automate. He continued to work at the VA, which he enjoyed very much due to the exposure to the many changes in technology. He was also serving as a deacon that required time and service in the leadership of his church, but he was sure he could find time to computerize Tom's machine. There was a lot to figure out and research, with many nights and weekends taken up developing the plans, programming, and finding the right parts to make it all come together. When he first started, Paul had no idea that automating the longarm machine he and Mildred first saw at the State Fair would take five more years before it was finally ready for sale.

CHAPTER FOURTEEN

Automation

Paul knew that Tom made a very good quality longarm machine. He wanted to add a computer to the mix so that the quilter could direct the machine in every aspect. Computers execute commands in steps, so initially Paul used stepper motors, but they ended up not being accurate enough and were also very noisy. Drawing from his knowledge about CNC machines which Paul used to cut metal and are also used in some medical equipment that require specialized movement, he knew the use of servo motors would work better. Servo motors run using a specialized computer called a controller that gets continuous feedback from the motors' actual positions and constant corrections by the controller keep the motors where the computer expects them to be. The quilter would need to interact with a PC, and the PC would interface with the controller to create the motions of the machine head. Paul purchased a closed-loop servo control system from the Galil Company, and once everything was connected together, he found that the accuracy was remarkably better. This type of servo system cost much more than the stepper motors, but Paul's drive for perfection made them worth the extra cost.

One of the first things Paul wanted to develop was the stitch regulator. This would allow the hand-guided quilter to stitch evenly while moving the head across the quilt at any speed. When Paul brought up the subject of regulated stitching, Tom said this was impossible since hand guided machines were not precise enough to go back into the same holes they had just sewn. He was very surprised when Paul demonstrated to him how he could actually do it.

The first quilting program was written in Microsoft's QuickBasic which was DOS based. Paul's son David wrote this first program and also helped to create some of the early patterns. Initially, Paul wanted to call the program "Compu-Quilt," but later discovered this name was already being used by another software developer. A copyright lawyer suggested using his name in the product, so the name "Statler Stitcher" was born.

Paul went through many trials and errors trying to discover the recipe of mechanical parts and electrical pieces that would work together in the best way. If an idea was not working well enough, he had to give up on it and try something else. First he tried using cables instead of notched belts. The cable would slip while going around the pulley causing inaccuracies in the stitching. The notched belt would only slip if the belt became loose, which was not likely. Paul was meticulous in wanting to make a machine that would sew as accurately as possible.

An early machine using the first iteration of DOS based software written by Paul's son David

One early attempt was to attach the motors from rails mounted up high above the table with the machine head hanging from the motors, but it just was not stable enough. Now the head has attached wheels that run on tracks fastened to the table. Initially, the first table was made of wood, but now it is made of metal. There were so many changes that had to be worked out, and thankfully Tom was very patient to allow Paul to get things right.

Paul bought an empty PC case, stripped it out, and put in the circuit boards he designed and wires which are connected to the controller that guides the movements of all three axis motors. The Galil servo controller converts the human's request (via the PC) into signals the motors can understand, such as commands to say how large a circle will be, or in other words, where to start and stop the arc. Most controllers like this are made for cutting metal and wood, not for stitching cloth. Paul's contact and friend at Galil, Kaushal Shah, Vice-President of the company, states that the use of their controllers for quilting is very unusual. Paul once presented Kaushal with a stitched quilt which is now hanging in his California-based office and states he is very proud of the use of their Galil equipment in Statler Stitcher machines.

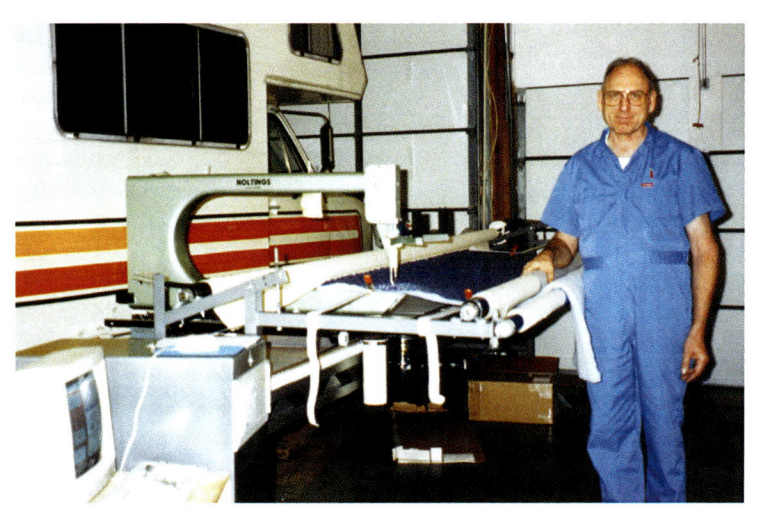

Because Paul's son David had moved out of town and could not devote as much time as needed due to being in the early stages of his new career as a systems programmer for the State of Missouri, Paul needed to find another programmer to create a new Windows-based program which would have a better user interface and more precise patterns. In 1993, he

64

hired Perry Ogletree who wrote the next iteration of software in Microsoft's Visual Basic which he called Stitcher Legacy Gold. It had a GUI (Graphical User Interface) with icons and areas for adjustments that the quilter could change for personalized stitching.

Thousands of actions within each process needed to be analyzed and reconstructed to automate the manual process of quilting. Thousands of dollars and man-hours were spent working through ideas trying to find what worked best. Many times Paul became discouraged during some of the failed attempts and thought it might be easier just to quit. Usually during these times, Paul's good friend Dave Jones would show up to encourage him to keep going. He would also try to help figure out the problem, but even more important to Paul was Dave's confidence in him. Paul believes this is why he tries to instill this same kind of confidence when training people, because he sees how important it was to him when he felt discouraged and wanted to give up.

David and Angie Jones and Family

Paul and Mildred have been very good friends with Dave and his wife Angie for many years and share a lot of common interests, such as tractor pulls and steam engine shows. Dave continually reminded Paul that he not put a product on the market until he believed it was perfect. Dave also helped in the early beta-testing of the machine as well. Paul states that he does not believe the Statler Stitcher would be here today without the help and encouragement from Dave when he needed it the most.

In 1990, Paul had the first fully functional Statler Stitcher machine up and running which Mildred used for her own personal quilts. It was also used for testing new patterns Paul created along with software updates.

Finally, after five years of research and development, trials and disappointments, much prayer, encouragement, accomplishments, and successes, Paul finally had a machine ready for Tom to begin selling in 1994.

CHAPTER FIFTEEN

Partnership

Throughout all this time, Paul continued to work at the VA hospital in Columbia. Even though he still enjoyed working there, his first retirement option became available since he was now age 55 with 30 years of military and VA work combined. After discussing with Tom what he thought about the chance of success, he assured Paul that it would be no problem to sell all of the computerized stitchers that could be built. Tom also stated that if Paul retired, he could take a more active role in the business by helping to deliver machines, and generally become more involved. He also told Paul that he had thirty people already interested in buying a computerized stitching machine.

Paul's retirement party at the VA Hospital, Columbia, MO

During the previous five years of development, Tom was very good about creating a bracket or any other part Paul needed and they got along very well. Everything was looking up and the timing seemed right, so Paul took early retirement, along with the subsequent cut in salary, in order to retire at the age of 55. Now fully dedicated to this endeavor, Paul was on his way.

About this same time, and unbeknownst to Paul, Tom obtained the services of an engineer named Richard "Dick" (not his real name) to reverse engineer and bypass the protection mechanism embedded in Paul's software. Just two weeks after Paul retired, he received a phone call from Dick, asking

66

various questions about the software. Paul did not recognize his name on the phone's caller id, and not knowing him personally, he asked Dick, "Did you purchase a machine?"

"No, " he replied and then continued, "Tom is paying me $10,000 to break the security code on your software." Paul was shocked and dumbfounded, first because this man was attempting to steal from him, and secondly because he was actually admitting to the fact.

Paul replied, "That's the same thing as stealing from me," but Dick did not seem to understand. "If you bought a brand new truck and I drove off with it, what would you do?" Paul asked. "I'd get the law after you," Dick replied. Paul responded, "Well, then I'd better sue you, because I care a whole lot more about this software than I do about a new truck. Besides, why are you calling me? Why are you talking to me?" Paul asked. "I don't know," Dick said. Paul responded, "Well, I guess I'll have to sue you."

And then Dick hung up.

Paul just sat there and was overrun with emotions, especially anger and frustration. He was deeply hurt by what just transpired. It was a Wednesday which is a regular church night for Paul and Mildred, so they attended as was their usual custom. In the middle of the sermon, the preacher stated, "When your business partner does you wrong, don't sue him, pray for him." This statement was completely out of context to the sermon he was preaching and after he said it, the pastor went back to what he was originally speaking about. He said nothing more about dealing with a business partner.

After the service was over, Paul approached a friend in attendance and asked if he had heard anything unusual in the sermon. He responded, "Yes, but I thought I had fallen asleep and missed something." Paul finally asked the pastor what he meant by what he said. After looking confused for a moment, he finally said, "I'm not sure why I said that."

Paul thought to himself that he knew why. It was the Lord directing him not to sue Tom. Paul had already purchased all of the parts needed to build ten computerized machines. He had used up most of his savings along with borrowed money. He had a lot of inventory, but very little money left. Plus, Tom owed Paul about $18,000, so if there was a lawsuit, he figured only the lawyers would be the ones to make any money from it. Therefore, Paul decided to go ahead with building the ten machines to recoup his investment. Paul never mentioned Dick's phone call to Tom, and just

Paul with one of his various attempts at trying something different - guiding the machine with a joystick

started working hard to build the new Statler systems, but included a small hardware change unique to each system to protect his intellectual property.

Paul would put a little soldered piece of wiring in different places on the circuit boards to accomplish this. He also disabled the connector so that when Tom tried to copy it, the machine and the software he made would not work. Paul knew Tom was building these other machines as every now and then he would receive a call about a machine that was not working. It would always be a call from someone not on Paul's list of purchasers. Because the machine carried his name, Paul would still go and fix the problem, even though he had not actually built that particular machine. Not long after, Paul learned that Tom went to Dick's house only to discover that there was a padlock bolted to the front door and no sign of him. Because of this and other problems with his "copycat" machines, Tom still came to Paul to buy his systems. The "partnership" continued on like this for awhile.

CHAPTER SIXTEEN

First Customers

The promotion and selling side of the business included going to trade shows and craft festivals. One of the first shows Paul attended with Tom was the Houston International Quilt Festival in November 1995. There were a lot of curious and interested people who visited the booth, but one of first actual buyers was Nadjerene "Nadj" Pankey who bought a longarm machine equipped with the computerized "Statler Stitcher" attachment.

Paul introducing his new machine at the Missouri State Fair which was initially named the "Statler Stitch"

A few months later, in January 1996, Tom and Paul delivered the actual machine that Nadj saw at the show to her new shop in Azle, Texas, a bedroom community of Fort Worth. The serial number on this machine was 54, which meant it was the fourth machine sold.

Upon setup of the machine, Tom mounted the computer on the right side of the machine instead of the left side where Nadj wanted it. Even after Nadj mentioned it, Tom would not hear of changing it. Due to some problems with the first system, Tom agreed to exchange it for a whole new system a few months later. Before loading the replacement machine for delivery, Paul noticed that the computer was again attached on the right side. He reminded Tom of Nadj's request that it be mounted on the left side, but he just responded, "I don't care; I'm not changing it."

69

When they finally arrived at Nadj's shop, which was 680 miles one way, after unloading it and setting it up, she said, "The computer is on the wrong side." Once again, Tom stated he would not change it. This time, Nadj spoke up and said, "Then load it back on the truck, and give me my money back." Paul took Nadj aside and asked her to accept the machine for now and that he and Mildred would drive the twelve hours back to change it for her. She agreed. On the drive back to Missouri, Paul mentioned to Tom, "Your stubbornness is going to cost you your business."

A similar situation happened during a delivery to South Carolina. During the setup of the machine, Paul noticed that one of the pulleys was crooked which could possibly cause a belt to jump off during the stitching. Tom refused to fix it while they were there. When the machine owner called to say the belt was jumping off, Paul knew exactly what the problem was. Mildred and Paul drove the long trip down to Saint Matthews, South Carolina and exchanged both the belt and the pulley.

Paul giving a demo to prospective customers

It was very hard for Paul to deal with Tom's attitude toward the customers. He was really good at the engineering side of the business, but not so much with customer service.

During this whole time, Tom had paid back the $18,000 he owed Paul, and continued to buy the computerized machines from him. That allowed Paul to recoup the money he had invested in parts.

Tom once again hired another engineer to break Paul's software code and it did not take him long to discover what Paul had been doing. This of course angered Tom and he called up Paul on the phone. He was talking real fast and called Paul a lot of names. After waiting until Tom had no more to say, Paul simply responded, "Tom, I was just protecting my invention. I am simply protecting my intellectual property." That conversation basically ended their relationship, both business-wise and personally.

Paul tried without success contacting other longarm quilting machine companies to see if they would sell him machine heads to customize. As it was now, without a source for heads, he could not make his Statler Stitcher available to customers, which also meant no income. The various companies felt that Paul was in direct competition to their hand-guided machines and would not sell to him. He even went to see Ken Gammill, the owner of the largest quilting machine business. Because his wife was a hand-guided quilter, she was not interested in the computerization of their system.

With no source of machine heads to computerize, Paul was basically out of work. He finally told Mildred, "We'll just start quilting," and they did.

CHAPTER SEVENTEEN

The Guild

With the building and selling of stitcher machines on hold, Paul decided to join a local quilt guild, but did not know it was a hand-quilting only guild.

At one of the first meetings he attended, Paul noticed he was one of only two men there. When it came time for introductions, he got up and introduced himself as a computer-guided longarm quilter. Right away he noticed a lot of frowns on some of the faces.

After the meeting, three leaders of the guild came up to Paul to straighten him out. "You can come to our meetings," they told him, "but don't talk about your computerized quilting machine. We're loyal hand-quilting quilters only, and this is a hand-quilting guild."

"I'm just here to learn more," Paul responded to them.

About four months later, Paul went once again to a guild meeting and brought along a whole cloth quilt that was 110 inches square and had very detailed stitching which was quilted on his Statler Stitcher machine at home. When it came time during the meeting for "Show and Tell," Paul just held up the quilt and did not say a word. Someone asked him how he quilted it and Paul just responded with a smile on his face, "I can't tell you," and sat down.

Not long after, some of the guild members started bringing Paul their pieced tops to quilt on his Statler Stitcher. For the next year and a half, they had a good quilting business going and Paul and his computerized machine became more accepted at the guild. He continued to attend the guild meetings during this time to deepen his understanding of quilting techniques and terminology. The meetings also taught him first-hand what was important to quilters which Paul incorporated into making the Statler Stitcher a better machine.

Paul tried working with various techniques to see if he could modify it for more efficiency. One such attempt was by injecting stuffing into a finished quilt. Another experiment was trying to make chenille. Paul thought chenille bed covers were very nice, so he created a special presser foot for laying down the yarn in patterns he designed.

Paul and Mildred were having a hard time keeping up with the demand for the whole-cloth quilts they were making, so he tried various ways to keep the machine running continuously. During one particularly busy week, Paul was falling behind on getting the quilts done before the Monday shipping deadline. During the weekend, he worked all day Saturday until late in the evening. Sunday morning before leaving for Sunday School, he put in a new bobbin and started the machine. Since it took about an hour to sew a row, after Sunday School Paul returned home, rolled the quilt, put in a new bobbin, started the machine again, and returned to church for services. After church, he returned home again, rolled the quilt, put in a new bobbin, started the next row, and left to go out to eat lunch. After lunch, he returned and continued to sew more quilts throughout the rest of the day. Needing to work through the night to complete the order, he had to find a way to wake up every hour to advance the quilt. Paul did not want to set the alarm to keep waking Mildred up every hour, so he drank a quart jar full of water before laying down relying on "Nature's Call" to wake him about every hour. He would then put in a new bobbin and advance the quilt. Paul continued this throughout the night and got all of the quilts finished and shipped out Monday morning.

They were selling the majority of the quilts to Pat and Frank Fuchs who would resell them at various craft shows and fairs. Pat and Frank also became one of the early Statler Stitcher owners. Frank loved loading a quilt and then sitting back in his easy-chair to watch the machine do all the work.

Paul with his first grandchildren, Justin and Julian, twins, 1991

CHAPTER EIGHTEEN

Star of David Quilt

Judith Moore, a lady who attended the same church as Paul and Mildred, heard about how they were making quilts and approached them with an idea for a special pattern. She told them, "It's a vision I've received of the Star of David with a dove in the middle of it, and an olive branch in the dove's mouth. It came to me like a dream, along with the message, 'Those who bless Israel will be blessed.'"

Judith, along with another friend Marilyn Hargis, later visited Paul and Mildred at their house where they more fully discussed this pattern idea. Marilyn, who is neither a quilter nor an artist, took pen to paper and quickly drew out the pattern. She had drawn it without double stitching using the fewest lines possible, and gave it a 3-D effect. Paul then took the drawing and created a digital pattern from it for quilting on his machine. He created a few small sample quilt blocks, using olive leaves between the blocks. Judith and Marilyn liked it and commissioned Paul to make a full-sized quilt using these blocks to border the designed Star of David pattern.

Halfway through the quilting, the machine stopped working correctly. It would not pick up the bobbin thread and Paul could not figure out how to fix it. He eventually took the whole machine head to the senior repairman at Tom's factory. He said nothing was wrong with it as it sewed perfectly for him. Paul took it back home and loaded a different quilt on the machine, and it sewed just fine. Putting the Star of David quilt back on the machine, it refused to sew again. Paul fought this problem for two weeks and finally put the quilt aside, unfinished.

In 1996, Paul and Mildred had attended a revival service at the Brownsville Assembly of God church in Pensacola, Florida. At the time, people from all over the world were coming to this special revival and people would get in line outside the church beginning at 4 o'clock in the morning to be able to get a seat for the 7 p.m. service. Paul and Mildred were one of the last to get into the sanctuary building that night and sat high in the balcony with the rest of the people sent to the overflow area in the gymnasium. There was a wonderful time of worship and the sermon was powerful. Afterwards, Paul purchased one of the church's worship music CD's, which they would listen to now and then.

After a time, and for reasons unknown, Paul decided to try working on the Star of David Peace quilt once more. He wanted some background music while quilting, so he picked out and began playing the revival's worship music CD. When he started the machine, it began sewing perfectly. It picked up the bobbin thread without any problems. When the CD got to the end and stopped playing, the machine also stopped sewing as the bobbin started having the same problem again. But when Paul restarted the CD, the machine began to work just fine. Any time Paul would stop the CD from playing this praise music, the machine would just not sew right. So Paul kept the music playing until the quilt was finished.

Judith was a member and teacher with the End-Times Handmaidens and Paul decided to donate the Star of David quilt to the organization for a fundraiser auction during their annual meeting held in 1997 at their headquarters in Arkansas. The auction went late into the early morning hours of the next day, and the quilt never came up for sale, but the miraculous story of how the quilt was made was shared with those still in attendance. A lady at the auction stated she had a vision and desired that the quilt be anointed and taken to Israel.

Paul holding up the Star of David Peace quilt

Therefore, it was decided by the group to not sell it to an individual, but instead they prayed over the quilt, anointing it as a gift of peace and determined a way for it to be delivered into the hands of Israel's Prime Minister, Benjamin Netanyahu. Merrie Turner, who was attending the auction, would be returning to Washington, D.C. in a few days and had plans to attend an event where Benjamin Netanyahu and his wife would also be in attendance, and thought she could present the quilt to them at that time.

Before attending the event, she was impressed by God to wear a special dress of the Colonial American period that she had sewn years before. Although she did not think it would be appropriate to wear this type of dress to the event, she felt God was leading her to wear the colonial ball gown of white taffeta, with black and blue taffeta trim.

Gwen Shaw (right), head of the End-Time Handmaidens

74

The plane carrying the Prime Minister and his wife to the United States was late arriving, and due to the event being cut short, the quilt was not able to be formally presented to them. After the event, Mrs. Netanyahu spotted Merrie dressed in her colonial ball gown. Piquing her curiosity, Mrs. Netanyahu made her way over to Merrie to inquire about her dress. This provided Merrie with the opportunity to explain about the Star of David quilt and present it as a gift to Mrs. Netanyahu and the Prime Minister, which she agreed to accept on her husband's behalf.

An official letter dated February 1, 1998 was received from the Prime Minister's office to the End-Time Handmaidens organization stating his thanks for the beautiful quilt which was presented to him and Mrs. Netanyahu. Paul and Mildred have a copy of this letter hanging on their wall as a reminder that, "with God, all things are possible," (Matthew 19:26). A wall hanging of the Star of David pattern along with a copy of the letter was sent to Jacob Tal, who was born in Israel and founded Galil, Inc., which he hung proudly in their headquarters.

After this, the doors of opportunity and business opened wide. While Paul was doing mainly quilting, he was also researching and upgrading his stitcher machine and had upgraded to a newer control system. Paul approached Ken Gammill once again, asking to buy a machine head and table without any motors or wiring for his own personal use. Ken sold him one and now Paul had the original machine he had bought from Tom which was equipped with a Statler, plus now had his first Gammill that would have a Statler attached to it.

Closeup of the Star of David quilt block

Some of the other quilting machine companies also became interested in having Paul retrofit their hand-guided machines with the computerized Statler Stitcher. So many things changed after making the Star of David Peace quilt that Paul often ponders just how important it was for him to follow through with finishing it.

75

CHAPTER NINETEEN

Kim Diamond and the First MQS

After meeting Paul during one of the local quilt guild meetings and seeing the wholecloth quilts he had made, Kim Diamond was invited to view a demonstration at Paul's house of what his machine could do. Realizing the possibilities of what she could do, she enthusiastically stated, "I want that machine!" Paul responded, "That's Mildred's machine, but I'll make you one though." Kim reiterated that she wanted that machine and that he could make Mildred another one. After further discussion, Paul relented and Kim got her machine, which was the first official Gammill Statler Stitcher.

At a later guild meeting, Kim asked Paul if he was going to Springfield. "What's in Springfield?" he asked. "Machine Quilters Showcase, which is a specialized show for machine quilters, led by Marcia Stevens. You need to go," she responded.

MQS, started by Marcia and her husband Tom, was the first show dedicated to the unique system of machine quilting that utilizes a track system. In 1998, they moved the show from Duluth, Minnesota to Springfield, Missouri to be more centrally located.

Kim Diamond

Finding a longarm quilting e-mail list on the Internet, Paul joined the list, introduced himself, and presented an overview of his computerized system and what it could do. He received a lot of emails with questions about it, including one from Marcia Stevens, asking if he would like to be a vendor at the MQS event in Springfield. The event was only four days away, so Paul thought it was too late to get anything together for the show. Additionally, he had no hotel reservation and thought it would cost thousands of dollars for a vendor booth. Initially excited about the opportunity, it just seemed impossible to get everything ready in time. The next day after Sunday morning church services, Paul and Mildred went out to lunch with Judith Moore and the topic of MQS was brought up. After Paul mentioned about his invitation, but deciding not to attend due to time constraints, Judith spoke up and said, "Paul, you can do this!"

As they were sitting there, a gentleman by the name of Dave that Paul knew sat down at a table near them. Knowing he was in the business of making videos, Paul explained the situation and asked him if he had time to make a video for him to show at MQS. Dave explained that he was completely booked with graduation and wedding videos, but if he could do it right after lunch, he would have time to fit it in. Dave came to Paul's house and filmed footage for a demonstration video that same afternoon and delivered a professionally edited video to him Monday morning.

Judith helped by creating a brochure Paul could hand out at the booth with highlights and pricing information about the machine. Paul contacted Marcia Stevens about not having a reservation. She said she always holds a few hotel rooms back for just such emergencies, and she also only charged Paul $375 for an 8 x 10 foot booth. This was plenty of room for displaying a few quilts, including another Star of David Peace quilt, and a sample of the whole-cloth quilt he had designed. There was also enough room for setting up a projector to show his new video. Excited how it all came together so quickly, Paul and Mildred had to get up at 4 a.m. Wednesday morning to get to Springfield in time for the show.

During that Springfield MQS show, Paul sold two retrofits (where the Statler Stitcher is added to an already existing hand-guided machine). One of these went to Michigan and the other to California. Paul mailed out the kits with detailed instructions and a new video he had created to show how to put it all together. To Paul, it seemed like another miracle had taken place in how all the pieces came together so quickly to attend the show, along with the added bonus of selling two systems.

Because Paul had sold his original Gammill machine to Kim, he had to go back to Ken Gammill to buy another one. Ken had never seen the Statler in action, but was very interested in seeing how it worked. On Ken's next visit to Columbia, Paul contacted Kim Diamond and drove Ken over to her house to see the machine. When they got to her house, she was outside getting the mail. They followed her inside, where the machine was quilting away by itself. Ken was amazed and very impressed.

Kim Diamond and Paul Statler

After seeing what this machine could do and envisioning the possibilities for the future, Ken offered Paul a contract for them to work together. Reviewing the contract, Paul determined that it was a little out of balance between them profit-wise, so he refused it. Ken then agreed to sell Paul basic quilting machine heads which allowed Paul to sell the machines fully equipped with the Statler Stitcher.

Excited to show off this new system, Ken went to a quilt show in Tacoma, Washington and took one of Paul's machines to sell. While unloading it, he dropped the cross-track motor which caused it not to work so he could not show it. After Paul repaired the motor, Ken took the machine to a show in Houston, Texas and dropped the computer which cracked the motherboard causing it not to work. After those incidents, Paul thought it might be easier to just sell the Gammill machines with the Statler Stitcher attachment himself. Ken agreed and stated it would also be okay for Gammill dealers to work with him if they so desired. Paul was back in business.

Paul at a show booth in Atlanta, GA 1994

A little time later, Paul bought back that second Gammill machine from Ken which he fixed up and eventually sold to his next door neighbor. That machine ran continuously with all original parts until recently when the controller was damaged from lightning.

CHAPTER TWENTY

Changing Hands of the Prototype

When Paul had sold his first Gammill machine to Kim Diamond in 1998, she took over most of his quilting business. He also taught her how to design her own patterns. Since Paul was the world's first computerized pattern designer, he personally taught most of today's top pattern creators on the art and technique of design.

By 1999 Paul had pretty much stopped quilting altogether as the selling of machines had really taken off. The first machine Paul had bought from Tom, the prototype, was still in his possession. Because he had developed a newer control system, the prototype had become outdated, even though it still ran fine. Paul and Mildred still used it a lot, but they needed the space for assembling the newer machines. Paul contacted Pat Fuchs and inquired if she had an interest in buying this used machine and offered to sell it to her.

Although Pat did not want to buy it for herself, her sister Teresa "Terri" Hansen did as she was in the market for a used Statler machine. She lived on a ranch in Texas at the time so Paul and Mildred made the trek to deliver the machine, set it up, and to give Terri all the training she could absorb. Because this was the first machine Paul had made, it came with all of his original patterns. When he sold it to Terri, Paul told her that she could have all of these original patterns he created, but she could not give them to anyone else. The patterns were accessed via Microsoft Word and to make adjustments to them, a "Stitcher Program Manager" software program running under Microsoft Windows 3.11 was used.

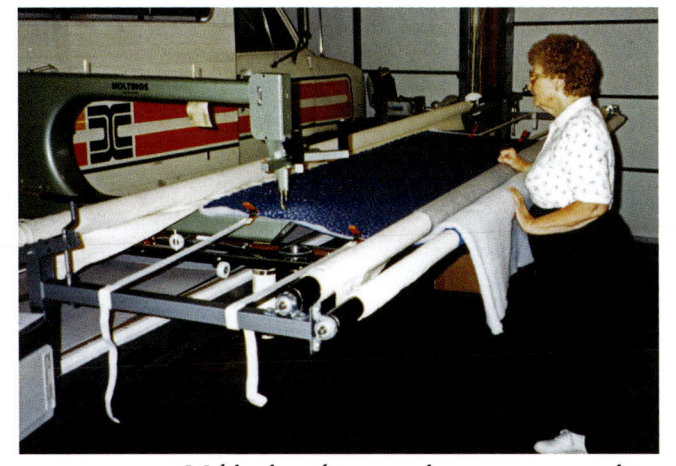

Mildred quilting on the prototype machine

Terri has used the machine many years creating quilts, and taking the time to teach neighbor girls along with her own granddaughter the love of sewing and quilting. Due to back injuries sustained in a car accident in 2005, Terri is not able to use the machine any longer, but refuses to sell it even though it takes up a whole room. She states, "I just couldn't. It is more than just a quilting machine. Paul invented something that no one had done before and it made everyone's life so much easier. This machine is his baby. It's the first! It is his prototype! It probably belongs in a museum."

CHAPTER TWENTY-ONE

It is all in the Details

Paul states that there were a lot of struggles getting the business started. He was breaking ground in an area no one else had yet ventured. There were many obstacles along the way, not only with technology, but also the resistance from hand quilters.

Computers consistently change and improve which means updates have to be made to the software to make sure the quilting systems continue to function properly. Starting with the DOS operating system, every command had to be entered sequentially which slowed everything down. Research began years ago, starting when Paul was still working at the VA hospital and has continued ever since.

Originally, the software commands sent signals to an amplifier, enabling them to run a motor. Paul experimented with many different ways to get the motor-driving circuits to work, spending time on nights and weekends, to get the perfect combination of power and speed in the motors. The machine has not just one motor, but three. One runs the needle up and down, and the other two determine the coordination of the x-axis with the y-axis.

After that first visit with Tom in his booth at the Missouri State Fair, where Paul first saw the longarm, later that night while spending the night in their motorhome, Paul began figuring out the x and y motor system he started with. He based it on his experience at the hospital with computer controlled X-ray machines and CAT scanners. These types of medical equipment have to be very precise, so dealing with the repairs of these machines gave Paul a good background in dealing with these types of motors.

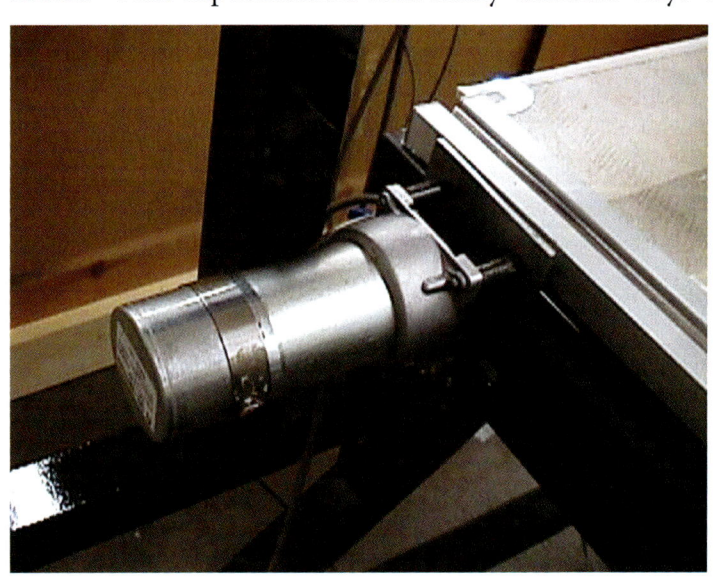

Servo Motor

The accuracy Paul was able to obtain with the motors was very precise, but due to the movement and stretching of the quilt fabric during the sewing process, there was a lack of accuracy in the stitching. Paul was disappointed by this as he was not able to overcome this issue totally.

Storage of the software also evolved from floppy disks, to CD's, to DVD's, to website downloads. The computer's operating system continues to upgrade causing changes to firmware, software, and other components as well. Using a notched belt he was able to get the machine to move better from left to right. He moved away from a stepper motor to a servo motor which was more accurate and less noisy, but more expensive. Because the research and programming of the software was expensive, to protect his investment, he installed a security key on the system. Paul has always strived to build the best machine that he could.

Notched Belt

Ever since the day Paul saw Tom's factory in person, and its resemblance to his continual dream, he felt strongly that he was following the right path. Tom's betrayal was very painful, but Paul believes that the Statler Stitcher would not be what it is today without that original partnership.

While the machine, components, and software have all been important, nothing has been more important to the success of his business than the customers. From the very beginning, Paul believed listening to his customers was very important. He wanted not just to sell them something, but also serve them and meet their needs.

Paul in his booth at the 2000 MQS show

CHAPTER TWENTY-TWO

Off and Running

Once the dealers began selling the Statler Stitcher, things really began to take off. Paul would assemble the computerized parts and attach them to the Gammill machine head and then run each machine through a burn-in period of 24 hours straight. The dealer would usually come to Paul's house where they would run them through a quality assurance check once more to verify they were in good working order. Paul and the dealer would then dismantle the machine, load it into their van or truck, and then the dealer would proceed to deliver, install, and be responsible for training the customer on their new investment. Paul would remain responsible for any parts that needed replacing under warranty, but the dealer was responsible for any routine maintenance.

Paul was still working and selling machines from his home during this time, and because the business was growing so fast, he decided to add on to the house, building a large shop on the northwest end. He then had a loading dock added to the front of the house, where trucks could back up and unload their deliveries. The Statler household is probably the only residence in Columbia with a loading dock. A total of 3,000 square feet was added to the original house that could be used for the Statler business.

Paul hired Harold "Harry" (not his real name) in 2001 to help take care of the financial side of the business which Paul did not really like to work in much. Harry was very sharp and knowledgeable with computers as well, and did a really good job keeping the books.

After Mildred's step-father passed away from Parkinson's disease in 2001, her mother

Mildred, Arlene, and Jewel Blansett
2007

82

Arlene moved in with Jewel, Mildred's brother, who was living in Jefferson City, Missouri at the time. After developing some health problems, she had to be moved to a nursing home. Arlene passed away in January 2009 at the age of 96.

Paul and Mildred began to worry that the neighbors might start complaining about the number of trucks coming by the house making deliveries, so they began looking for a warehouse close to town. In 2002, Paul found a warehouse just east of Columbia that was the perfect fit for the business and could also accommodate the predicted growth. The new space allowed Paul to set up demonstration machines from each of the five main machine head companies, each running with the attached Statler. Practically 100 percent of customers bought the Gammill brand when comparing machines in this way. They are a true industrial machine, built stronger and with better tables.

Mildred and Paul in front of the new Statler Stitcher shop

There was the time when none of the manufacturers wanted even to speak to Paul about his machine, but now that a successful, tried and true computerized option was on the market, they all wanted in on it. And Paul wisely agreed to equip their machines with the Statler attachment.

Paul was buying computers ten to twelve at a time, on a pallet from the local Sam's Club. Once, the manager asked him what he was doing with all those computers. Paul replied that he made computerized quilting machines. The manager remarked that his wife was a quilter and Paul just smiled. Mildred customized each of the PC's by loading the necessary software needed to run the computerized machines. Wiring, inventory items, motors, parts, and pieces were always on order to fulfill the continual demand of dealers' orders. Paul also took orders at the various quilt shows and expos, where the Statler was demonstrated.

Before each machine left the shop, it was fully tested. Paul would stretch out a roll of butcher paper between the rollers to test patterns. The needle would punch holes in the paper, and if everything was working right, during a second time of running the pattern, the needle would come down in the very same holes. He would run an edge-to-edge pattern as much as five times, and only have one set of holes due to the accuracy of the Statler. Thread tension was tested using real fabric.

With business really picking up and staying so busy with trying to meet all of the orders from dealers and new customers, it became apparent that Paul and Mildred needed to hire more help, including someone who could also stay at the shop while they were traveling.

After much prayer for direction, one day Dave Kapka just arrived at their front door and was an answer to those prayers. Dave had previously owned a bicycle shop, and lived next door to a lady who owned a Statler Stitcher. He had actually spent some time quilting on her machine and understood the maintenance aspect of it as well. While visiting the Statler shop, Dave helped to build the next machine Paul was going to deliver and stayed on as an actual employee after that.

Paul and Mildred began praying again for someone with a mechanically oriented background. Bob Simpson, a friend from church who had recently retired and moved to Florida with his wife, was back visiting family in Missouri. Attending church that Sunday, he sat down by Paul and Mildred and visited with them before the service started. Paul thought to himself that this is someone who could come and help them. So after church Paul asked Bob if he would be willing to move back to Columbia and come work for him. He just laughed and said, "No way." Even though Bob himself was keen on the idea, he was pretty sure he would not be able to convince his wife to move from the new house they had built in Florida. On the following Wednesday, Bob called Paul and said his wife would consider returning to Missouri only if she could get her old house back.

Of course, their previous house had been sold, but talking to the owners, they were willing to sell it back to the Simpsons. So Bob and his wife returned to Columbia and he began working for Paul. Another prayer had been answered.

It was not long before the production of machines was falling behind once again due to increasing sales. Whenever this happened, Paul and Mildred would start praying for an answer to the need. An acquaintance who had worked for the University joined the team and was just the right person at the right time. He designed and built the circuit boards for the system.

In 2003, another answered prayer was Dennis Engdahl, who came along just as they were trying to upgrade the software. While vacationing in Missouri, he had called Paul about getting a retrofit for his wife's quilting machine. He was also a recently retired professor of computer science and was looking for "something to do." Paul offered to give Dennis and his wife a retrofit in exchange for his programming assistance, and he agreed. The PrecisionStitch software was born from this agreement, with the name suggested by Paul after seeing a man with a work shirt that had the word "precision" stamped on the back. "Precision Stitching with quality, that's it!" Paul said. Dennis wrote several solid upgrades for the program over the next few years. He was another person God used in the Statler story to fulfill the needed task.

Later that year, Galil, the maker of the controller circuit boards used in the Statler machines, recognized Paul and his team as a "Smart Moves Partner." They presented Paul with a plaque along with writing an article about the Statler Stitcher in a company promotional publication.

CHAPTER TWENTY-THREE

Special Deliveries

The wonderful employees at the Statler Stitcher warehouse kept the machines coming while Paul and Mildred made the deliveries, attended the quilt shows, and serviced their customers' machines. Paul bought a motorhome specifically for making the deliveries, which had plenty of space for hauling the machines and the conveniences of being at home.

Their first trip with the motorhome was to South Carolina. It was in March and when they got to the Appalachian Mountains, it started snowing so hard they had to stop for the night at a truck stop. In the morning, they followed a snow plow to get down out of the mountains.

On another delivery trip out west, they had six machines loaded up in the motorhome. With the heavy load and going over the mountains, they had a problem with the engine vapor locking. Paul would just pour water over the fuel pump to get going again. After that trip, Paul had a mechanic put a racing engine in the motorhome and no longer had any problems taking it out West except for keeping it under the speed limit.

One memorable trip to the East Coast was to a customer in New York who found out about the Statler Stitcher over the Internet. They ordered the Supreme model with the largest table size, 22 feet long, which was loaded into the 27 foot motorhome through a window. Paul and Mildred stayed the night outside of New York City, so they could time their drive into the city and be at the delivery address by 6 a.m. to avoid rush hour traffic. The delivery was to a warehouse on the fifth floor of a downtown New York City building. The customer needed the larger table size to create stage curtains and backdrops for Broadway plays along with blankets for circus elephants. One problem to overcome was that the long table would not fit in the elevator. The top of the elevator was then removed to fit the table and get it up to the fifth floor. After finally getting the table setup and the training completed around midnight, the customer took Paul and Mildred up to the roof of the building where ten to twelve city blocks could be seen, including the Twin Towers. It was an amazing sight to behold. Leaving after midnight, they still got stuck in traffic, as New York City never truly sleeps.

After later having some mechanical problems with the motorhome, Paul bought a conversion van along with a specially made trailer to hold the tables that earned a number of nicknames such as the "Silver Bullet" and the "Flying Coffin." The trailer was long and low enough that Paul could see over it to view the cars behind him. Due to its unique shape, people at gas stations would ask Paul what he had in the trailer. He would usually respond, "I loved my mother-in-law so much that I couldn't part with her. So I just haul her around with me." They would usually do a double-take on the "coffin" and then usually figure out he was kidding. Many trips were made in the van with the "Silver Bullet" following behind.

One of the early trailers used to haul machines

One delivery brought another unique challenge. Arriving at the address, a woman opened the door of her home and said, "Hi, Paul." Making their way through the house, Paul was worried about where the machine was going to go. The lady finally indicated that it was to go down in the basement where she had cleaned out a space for it. Because the staircase had a corner in it, there was no way to take the table downstairs. Thankfully, there was a small window in the basement which they could remove. After taking the table all apart, they were able to pass everything through the window into the basement and reassemble it.

Paul and Mildred with the newer "Silver Bullet" trailer
2001

Below: The trailer which was damaged from a tree
2012

CHAPTER TWENTY-FOUR

Corporate Ownership

In March of 2004, Ron Parker had recently been hired as the new CEO of Gammill. Paul regularly went to the Gammill headquarters in West Plains, Missouri to pick up machine heads which he converted to Statler machines. On one such visit, the new CEO cornered Paul and told him, "You know Paul, one of these days you're going to want to sell your company." A little taken aback, Paul responded, "I am?" Ron continued, "Yes, and when you are ready to sell your company, we are going to buy it."

Gammill itself had just been acquired at the end of 2003 by Fulham & Co., a private equity firm headquartered in Massachusetts. Ron, understanding that computerization was the future of the quilting industry, set his immediate focus on the acquisition of Statler Stitcher.

Paul had never really considered selling the company, but he had been planning for the future of it. Since he knew he would not be able to run it forever, he offered it to his son David, asking him if he would be interested in taking it over. After much prayer and consideration, David declined as he was still in the middle of raising a young family and had a very good job in Information Technology with the State of Missouri.

In July of 2004, Paul and Mildred went on a rare vacation, boarding an Alaskan cruise ship after being in Canada for customer training. It was very relaxing and they enjoyed the various sights and activities such as taking an airplane ride over the Alaska landscape, riding in a horse-drawn bus, and seeing the majestic whales. They even visited a quilt shop while docked in Victoria, Canada.

In October of 2004, Paul and Mildred attended Cindy Roth's training show in the state of Washington and even bought a new motorhome there, driving it back home. Later that month, they shipped six crates of Statler machines to Kay and Bruce Brown, dealers in Australia, making a deal with them that when they had sold ten machines, Paul and Mildred would themselves come and give personalized training. This was just one example of how the Statler business was growing and expanding to other parts of the world.

Left: Paul giving a demo at Cindy Roth's training show in Washington
Right: Paul and son-in-law Tim preparing the crates to be shipped to Australia

All along, since that first meeting in March, Ron continued to meet with Paul, trying to convince him how selling the business to Gammill would help to increase his and Mildred's leisure time and would entail fewer responsibilities. By this time, with the building of machines, selling, delivery, training, and picking up new machine heads, Paul and Mildred were each putting in 80 hour work weeks. Even with the help of the other employees, Paul felt he just could not put in the time needed for further research and design development, the side of the business he really loved. Therefore, by November, Paul sat down in serious negotiations with Gammill for the selling of his business.

After obtaining guidance from attorneys on both sides, Paul negotiated three requests with the selling of the company: 1) The current employees would be respected and properly cared for; 2) Future upgrades to the software would always be free to the Statler owners; and 3) The kind of customer service he believed in would continue into the future.

Gammill also wanted Paul to stay involved and offered him a consulting agreement. Ideally, Ron wanted it to be a lifetime deal, but Paul was offered one, three, or five years with his option to pick. "Let's start with five years," Paul responded. Ron wanted only two or three days a week out of Paul, but due to Paul's work ethic and dedication, both he and Mildred continue to work more than full time. They can even be found most evenings at home working in their "garage" factory cutting wires, creating parts, and assembling circuit boards. Every Statler Stitcher assembled contains parts that Paul and Mildred have personally made.

Mildred working at home in the garage

On December 31, 2004, meeting with Gammill in the business office at the Statler factory in Columbia, Paul and Mildred signed the papers to hand the reigns of the Statler Stitcher Company over to Gammill, Inc. Coming out of the office, the employees were all called together and Angelo Ciavarella, the operating partner for Fulham, made the announcement. As Angelo was reassuring the employees that nothing was really changing, Paul remembers still seeing a few tears in their eyes.

CHAPTER TWENTY-FIVE

A New Beginning

Now with the day to day operations of the company under new management, Paul was able to devote more time on what he loved, such as developing new ideas to keep the Statler ahead of the competition and training new customers in the "World of Statler" throughout parts of the country and around the world.

As promised to the Browns, the dealers in Australia, that when they had sold ten machines Paul would come "down under" to personally train the new owners. Not only had the Browns sold those ten machines, but by the time Paul and Mildred finalized the schedule to come, they had sold twenty.

Arriving in Australia on February 15, 2005, Paul and Mildred stayed with Kay and Bruce Brown, who lived near Sydney. Kay made arrangements for the arriving trainees to stay in several homes near their studio and had made special Statler quilted quilts for everyone. The first group of trainees arrived on Sunday and training began on Monday morning. The day was dedicated to learning various techniques in the Precision Stitch software. They were also very interested in the AutoSketch program, so on Tuesday Paul gave instruction on that.

Bruce and Kay Brown with Paul and Mildred

Paul giving instruction to a group of trainees

A second group of trainees came later in the week and Paul covered it all a second time with them.

One slight challenge for Paul was the difference in the use of words in Australia. While working with Bruce Brown on fine tuning one of the machines, he asked Paul to "put a torch on it." Paul thought he wanted to burn something, or put a match to something, but Bruce was simply asking for a flashlight. To Paul, driving on the "wrong" or left side of the road seemed like an impossible task. When Bruce asked Paul if he would like to drive, he simply said, "No," and got in on the left, the passenger side. During their visit to the Sydney Zoo, Mildred got to pet a kangaroo and a koala along with getting see a baby kangaroo in its mother's pouch.

On the weekend before leaving, Bruce took Paul on a plane ride over parts of Australia including flying over the coal mines where Bruce once worked. They also visited a fabric shop located up in the mountains where the owners recognized Paul and Mildred from their pictures on the Internet. On Sunday morning, they attended church with the Browns in Sydney. That evening, they asked Kay and Bruce if they could attend the Hillsong church, which began in Australia and is now widely known with sister churches in New York, London, Kiev, Moscow, and other locations around the world. That evening happened to be the church's youth night, so the music was loud and lively and was a wonderful memory for the Statlers.

Outside of Hillsong Church

After the sale of Statler and before leaving for Australia, Paul was tasked with finding his replacement as "boss" for the Columbia shop. He chose the business manager, Harold, for the position.

Ron Parker presented a couple of candidates for hiring an in-house programmer to work full-time on the software. After meeting with Paul, Matt Sherman accepted the position and started at the shop on March 1, 2005. He was an immediate asset getting right to work by making updates to the current PrecisionStitch program. One of his first assignments was to have the software sew alternating patterns which would allow every other row to be offset from the one ahead of it and to have it ready before the next MQS show which was coming up in a few weeks. Until then, there was no office coffee pot at the Statler shop because Paul did not care for the smell. Since Matt was a coffee drinker, he asked Paul that if he got the alternating patterns project done before MQS, could he then have a coffee pot and Paul responded that he could. Working diligently, he

Matt Sherman

met the deadline, got his coffee pot, and made many other useful improvements to the PrecisionStitch software over the following months.

About two weeks before Paul and Mildred were to leave on a group tour of Israel, their daughter Mary gave birth to their granddaughter Bethany Rose on March 14, 2005 bringing their total number of grandchildren to nine.

The trip to Israel was sponsored by the End Time Handmaidens organization and was a very special and meaningful trip to Paul and Mildred. Paul was asked to help with baptisms in the Jordan River. He would help bring the people to be baptized down into the water, guide them to the preacher, and then help bring them back up out of the water. Paul felt truly honored to help with the baptism of people in the same river where Jesus was baptized.

They also visited other significant places such as the Wailing Wall and the Dead Sea. The group was once traveling to a particular site via a bulletproof bus when a big flash of light shown through the windshield. Someone from up on a bluff above the bus had thrown a Molotov cocktail bomb. Thankfully it hit the grill causing no damage and the driver just kept going, but it was a little frightening to those on board.

After returning home from Israel, Paul, Mildred, and the Statler crew headed to MQS in Overland Park, Kansas where he would be teaching and manning the Gammill vendor booth. They brought a machine into the main building and double-checked to make sure it would fit in the elevator since the classroom was the next floor down. About an hour before class time Kim Diamond, along with Paul, began to roll the machine into the elevator. What they did not know was that Ron Parker had put a new pivot access on the machine during the show which caused it to stick out six inches farther than when they had measured it. Since it now was not going to fit in the elevator, they pushed the machine back outside, onto the street, through some traffic down to the double doors on the lower level of the building. There was a single door unlocked there, but not the double doors needed to get the machine inside. Since it was about time for class to start, Mildred went to get the laptop so Paul could begin teaching and left Kim and Matt to find a way to get the machine into the classroom. After class was over, Bruce Brown, Matt, Paul and Mildred had to push the machine back up the street to the upper level doors of the building. It was also very windy that day and the loaded quilt was catching the wind like a sail making it hard to maneuver. They look back and laugh about it now.

Paul floating in the Dead Sea

The MQS show went very well, but a few weeks after arriving back home, Paul, Mildred, and their family experienced a tragic personal loss. On May 22, their new ten week old granddaughter Bethany passed away. The whole family was devastated and it was a very hard loss for them.

A few weeks later, on June 16th, Paul and Mildred left on a planned two-week tour of Europe prior to a scheduled machine installation in Belgium. They visited Austria, France, London, and Germany where they were able to locate the place where the original Statlers (originally spelled Stadler) lived along with discovering where one of their ancestors fought and died in a war. In London they saw the Big Ben tower and rode the London Eye, Europe's tallest Ferris wheel. They visited the Eiffel Tower after arriving in Paris. After their visit in Paris, they rode "the Bullet," a very fast train, to Belgium.

Bethany Rose Foley

The machine to be installed in Belgium had been pre-delivered and the crate had to be lifted up to a second story window by a crane to get it in the house. The machine was then set up and over the next few days, Paul gave training to the new owners. Even though both Paul and Mildred had a nice tour and visit in Belgium, they state that this trip is a little hard to remember since they were both still feeling so sad about the death of their granddaughter.

CHAPTER TWENTY-SIX

The Wreck

Later that year in October 2005, Paul had been cleaning up some land they had just purchased a month earlier and was heading home to pick Mildred up for lunch, but never arrived. He had called her a few minutes earlier to say he was "on his way and was just passing Wal-Mart." After waiting and waiting, and knowing it did not take that long to get to their house from Wal-Mart, Mildred knew something was wrong. She then got in her car and headed towards Wal-Mart. As she got closer, traffic was backed up and after finally reaching the intersection, she recognized Paul's car, wrecked and cut open. Now worried, she pulled off on the side of the road, and not seeing Paul anywhere, she located an officer and told him that it was her husband who had been driving the wrecked car. The officer told her that Paul had been taken to the hospital.

Paul had just passed Wal-Mart and was waiting at the intersection for the left-turn light to turn green. He was first in the turn lane and when the light changed, he began to pull out. A Chevy conversion van, going 55 mph and never touching the brakes, ran the red light and smashed into the side of Paul's Volkswagen Passat, spinning it around. Due to the excruciating pain caused by his injuries, Paul was going in and out of consciousness, but does remember someone at the window asking him if he was okay and was on a cell phone calling for help. The next time he woke up, he remembers riding in the ambulance, it being an awfully rough ride with a lot of pain, and blacking out again. The next time he awoke, technicians were taking X-rays to determine the extent of damage in his body. Paul was then taken to the ICU and he eventually woke up to very painful breathing. The doctors informed him that he had suffered seven broken ribs that had also punctured his lungs.

Mildred had finally gotten to the hospital and after receiving Paul's personal effects, she sat in the waiting room a long time until Paul was taken to ICU. Mildred called a close friend who came and sat and prayed with her. A doctor finally came out and informed her of Paul's condition and reassured her that his injuries were not life threatening even though Paul later stated he was not sure if he agreed with that assessment. Paul had to stay in the ICU about a week. Mildred's mother Arlene was staying with them at the time, so Mildred came home each night to be with her and returned to the hospital each day.

The main impact of the van had hit the hinge structure of the driver's side door and the wheel of the car. Paul's car was then knocked into the car next to him as well as the car behind it. Within seconds, four vehicles were totaled. It was later stated by the police that if Paul's car would have been just twelve inches further out into the intersection, he most likely would not have survived. As it was, firemen had to cut the car open to get Paul extracted.

Paul later learned that the driver of the van, a woman, was driving under the influence of drugs and speeding out-of-control through the red light. The situation was compounded by the fact that she was driving a borrowed vehicle, had a suspended license, and did not have insurance. After the accident, she also tried running away, but someone stopped her from leaving the scene.

Paul was eventually released from the hospital and spent the next several months recovering at home with the first few weeks being the worst. Still suffering from quite a bit of pain, the doctors prescribed Morphine to help deal with it. Knowing it to be an addictive painkiller, Paul did not take it very long and tried dealing with the pain in other ways. When the pain became unbearable, he would walk in a circle through the kitchen, into the sun room, through the living room, and around again until he was too tired to walk any farther. He would keep track of his "laps" by moving Cheerios from one small pile to another on the counter as he passed by. He did not move very fast, but after walking so far, and moving a certain number of Cheerios, he knew he would be able to rest again in the living room recliner which was the only place he could comfortably sleep. Paul would repeat this routine many times throughout each day.

As he healed, Paul had a lot of time to think, and contemplated a lot on what his mother taught him about being responsible for his own actions regardless of what others did to him. She would often say, "If you get angry, you will lose every time." Paul struggled with anger towards the woman acting so irresponsibly, but eventually was able to release that anger and completely heal mentally and spiritually, as well as physically. It is also a testament to Paul that even though he was in severe pain, he continued to work the long hours needed as he was able.

Earlier in the year, Paul and Mildred purchased a 100 acre tract of land east of Columbia which was close to the Statler shop. In the following months and years, they spent many hours clearing the land, enjoying the six acre lake stocked with catfish, and planting a small garden. They had small living quarters added to the existing pavilion where they have spent many nights during the weekends, restored the original barn, and remodeled a small farm house on the property. A spacious metal building located on the property houses their motorhome, tractor, other farm equipment, and a trailer used to haul wood. Paul and Mildred have invited many friends, church family, and groups of quilters who have come to the Columbia shop for training out to the farm for fun, food, fellowship, bonfires and hayrides.

Paul and Mildred's farm with restored barn and plenty of space for family, friends, and fun

Kim Diamond inquired of Paul when her machine should be updated, and in August 2005 delivered it to the Statler shop. Since this was the very first Gammill Statler machine Paul had sold, it was decided to make the "update" very special. After making a few mechanical updates, the machine head itself was sent to Quilt Center in Wisconsin to be given a new paint job, 18 layers of Candy Apple red paint. A silver plate with Paul's engraved signature was also affixed. Finally finished in December, Ron Parker

Kim Diamond with her new "Big Red" engraved with Paul's signature

of Gammill presented Kim with her new "Big Red," as he called it and Matt Sherman handed her a new can of car wax for keeping it polished. The metal plaque on it reads, "July 19, 1998 -- refurbished December 12, 2005."

CHAPTER TWENTY-SEVEN

Statler Congress and S.U.G.A.R.

At the MQS conference in May 2006, which was held in Overland Park, Kansas, Paul was awarded the "Lifetime Achievement Award" for his pioneering efforts in the area of computerized quilting and the invention of the regulated stitch. Paul spoke to the crowd of his incredible journey and how God's hand directed him throughout. His whole family was present to witness the ceremony.

Paul, Mildred, and family after receiving the MQS Lifetime Achievement Award

The first "Statler Congress" was held August 9-10, 2006, at the Statler shop in Columbia, Missouri, which brought together a large group of users to brainstorm new ideas and for Gammill to listen to their needs. Topics of discussion included what new features were desired or needed that the current software could not provide and what could be made better and easier to use. This team of users came up with many useful and innovative ideas. An e-mail account was created by Gammill to receive enhancement suggestions from users as well.

A second Statler Congress was held on May 10, 2007, where the first prototype version of the new software was previewed with users. Recommended changes were suggested along with more new ideas being submitted.

The new CreativeStudio software grew out of the Statler Congress meetings, users' suggestions, and Matt Sherman's creative genius, with version 1 of the software released on April 21, 2008. CreativeStudio was a total rewrite of the software code from the ground up which provided a better user interface, added the capability of pattern creation, and added a lot more options and features over the previous PrecisionStitch program.

Also in 2008, Kim Diamond organized a conference in Overland Park, Kansas for users of Statler machines, which was a huge success. At that conference, she expressed her desire to form an official user's group comprised by Statler owners. A group of volunteers came together to serve as a Board of Directors to help plan the next conference to be held in 2010.

Toward the end of December 2008, Paul and Mildred went to Moose Jaw, Canada to set up a machine and provide training for a new customer. At the hotel where they were staying was a very large indoor swimming pool. Paul noticed people coming through a partitioned area with "frozen" hair as it was standing straight up with frost on it. Paul jumped in the pool and discovered that going through the partition led to part of the pool that was outside. Since it was in the middle of winter, the temperature at the time was a minus 20 degrees, and girls with long hair would hold their wet hair up until it froze in that position. Paul later found out that the pool was heated by water pumped in from a natural hot spring located close to the hotel. When it was time for Paul and Mildred to leave Moose Jaw, there was a huge snowstorm which postponed their departure for three days. One problem was due to the door of the luggage compartment on the plane had frozen shut and could not be opened. This caused those who had just arrived unable to get their luggage and those waiting to leave not allowed to board. They were finally able to leave on December 22, arriving home just days before Christmas.

February 2009 marked the 50th Golden Wedding Anniversary for Paul and Mildred. A large group of family and friends came together to celebrate with them through a vow renewal ceremony and reception. Their children, David and Mary, escorted Mildred down the aisle and Paul's brother-in-law, Reverend Donald Blaylock, performed the ceremony. It was held at their home church, Christian Chapel, in Columbia, Missouri.

Celebrating Fifty Golden Years of Marriage

On July 27, 2009, Paul and Mildred arrived in Seoul, South Korea to set up a machine and give training. An organization that helps to provide activities to spouses of American military personnel bought a machine to provide quilting activities for those on base. An interesting part of the trip was that Paul was not allowed to give training to the Americans stationed there. He had to give the training to South Koreans, who would then in turn give the training to the Americans. There were, of course, some language barrier issues, but it all worked out in the end. Paul was able to privately teach one American lady after hours who became so excited about the Statler Stitcher that she purchased one after arriving back in the States.

At the second user conference held in Columbia, Missouri in June 2010, the attendees voted to officially form the user group, "Statler Users Group and Representatives," otherwise known as S.U.G.A.R. During that conference, Paul and Mildred were the recipients of the special "Lifetime Membership" award, given in appreciation of their dedication and perseverance to create the Statler Stitcher machine.

Paul and Mildred made another overseas trip to Bangkok, Thailand, arriving on April 26, 2011, to give training and help to a customer who had bought a machine there.

During the next S.U.G.A.R. conference's evening banquet, which was held in Columbia, Missouri in 2012, Paul was the focus of a surprise (to him) ceremony in the format of the old television show, "This is Your Life." Old photos of Paul were shown along with various stories told about him. Those that spoke included Ron Parker, Judith Moore, Kim Diamond, and Matt Sherman, along with special tributes given by his children, Mary and David. Jack Boersma even presented Paul with the old "Silver Bullet" trailer which was hidden behind a curtain in the ballroom.

Paul and Mildred with Mr. and Mrs. Ken Gammill

Another large influence in the Statler community has been an online mailing list which was initially called "Statler Sisters" that was started by Janice Bahrt. Even though the group name would infer that it only includes women, there are many men who are members as well. It is usually referred to as the "Statler Siblings" list today. Only verified Statler machine owners can join and membership is now well over 2,600. The list members help each other with hardware troubles, suggestions on pattern selection, sharing of quilting horror and success stories, giving usage tips and techniques, and coming up with suggestions for improvements of the Statler machine and software.

In 2013, Paul contacted a childhood friend who still lived in Sedgewickville, Missouri about obtaining a tractor. Jerry Ellis and his son restored old tractors and Paul asked if he could help him find an International Harvester Farmall B, which was the first tractor his father Coy had bought while on the farm. A short time later, Jerry contacted Paul to let him know he found a 1946 Type B in very good condition

Paul with his son David on the new Farmall Tractor.
Inset: Paul riding with his father Coy

98

(Paul's father's tractor was a 1944 Type B). Paul bought it and had the tractor delivered to his farm which now provides a source of joy and remembrance of the days on the old family farm.

Mildred had been having difficulty walking due to arthritis in her "Cotton Pickin' Knees," as she called them. In 2013, she had her right knee replaced and in 2014 had the left knee done. Recovery was tough, but Mildred's determination and knowing things had to get done gave her the strength to see it through and she did not let it keep her down very long.

In May 2014, while Paul was out mowing at the farm, Mildred received a phone call from one of her nephews stating that her brother Jewel was at the hospital in Osage Beach, Missouri. He had not been sick, but complained of having trouble breathing. His wife took him to the hospital, but he became unconscious before they arrived. The doctors tried to revive him but ultimately had to put him on a breathing machine. It became apparent after a few days that he would never wake up again. Paul and Mildred traveled down to the hospital and were there for support as Jewel's sons asked the doctor to unplug his machine, to allow him to pass. The funeral was held a few days later.

Jewel Blansett and his sons Kevin, Kent, and Keith

The 2015 S.U.G.A.R. conference was held June 18-20 at the Holiday Inn KC and KCI Expo Center in Kansas City, Missouri. Special attention given to highlight the 25th Anniversary of the Statler Stitcher. Videos of Paul with various machine owners were recorded to allow them to tell stories and give testimonies of how being a Statler owner changed their business and lives for the better. A special "photo booth" was also available where hundreds of pictures of Paul and Mildred with the attendees were taken. Special memorial T-shirts were made to mark the event as well.

On Thursday, September 10, 2015, the Gammill Company threw a surprise luncheon for Paul and Mildred at the shop in Columbia to help celebrate the 25th Anniversary of the Statler Stitcher.

Many of the employees from Gammill's headquarters in West Plains, Missouri were there along with Tim Fulham and Paul and Mildred's children. Tim presented Paul and Mildred with a plaque of appreciation and Paul spoke of how he got started in the business along with a few funny stories while a slideshow of old photos was shown.

Gammill employees and family gathered to celebrate 25 years of the Statler Stitcher

100

CHAPTER TWENTY-EIGHT

The Next Chapter

What is next for the Statlers? Only God knows for sure, but since the word "retirement" is not in Paul or Mildred's vocabulary, this is definitely not the last chapter but only the next step as they plan to continue to work with Gammill doing whatever needs to be done. To start with, Paul plans on traveling more to trade shows, conferences, training retreats, and quilt festivals working in the Gammill booth, providing training and sales, and of course giving out many more hugs and handshakes.

Paul saw an opportunity to create something useful. Not just for his wife, but for anyone willing to embrace it. He traversed various avenues, overcame many hurdles, and offered up a lot of prayer. That opportunity, through a combination of effort, determination, "Statler stubbornness," and help from family, friends, co-workers, and God, has been fulfilled and has greatly enhanced the lives of Paul and Mildred Statler. Through touching stories told to them daily from customers who have also become close friends, it has been very satisfying for Paul to see so many people benefiting from something he created.

Paul and Mildred's story is not yet finished. As long as they have breath and good health, they still have much to accomplish and live for. They are still leaders and ambassadors in the quilting world that have given new life and opportunities for success to countless people. They have nine grandchildren, to whom they have been a wonderful and godly example and they enjoy sharing their time, talents, and stories with them. Each one is unique and special in their own way, developing their own talents and futures as they are led by God. They have two children who still call upon them for guidance, direction, and an occasional helping hand to repair the kitchen sink faucet. Last but not least, they have each other, along with their strong faith in God. They are lifelong companions who support, love, encourage, strengthen each other, and have traveled more miles around the world together than most.

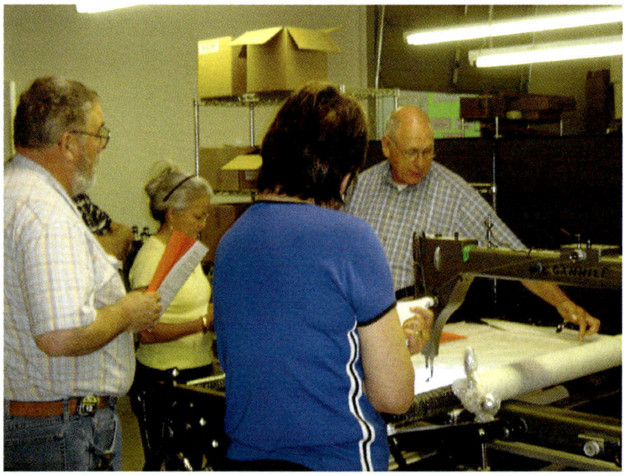

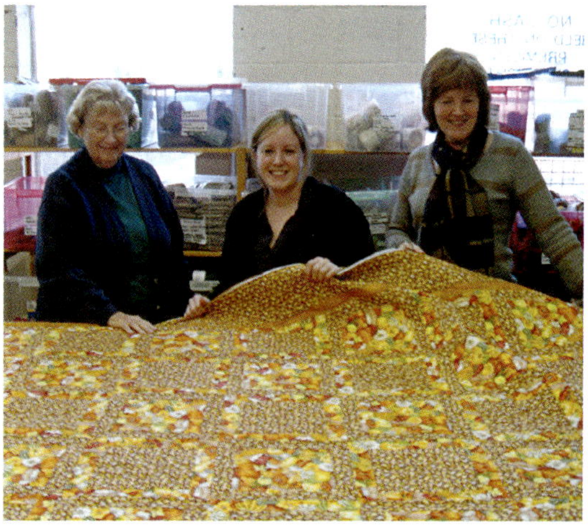

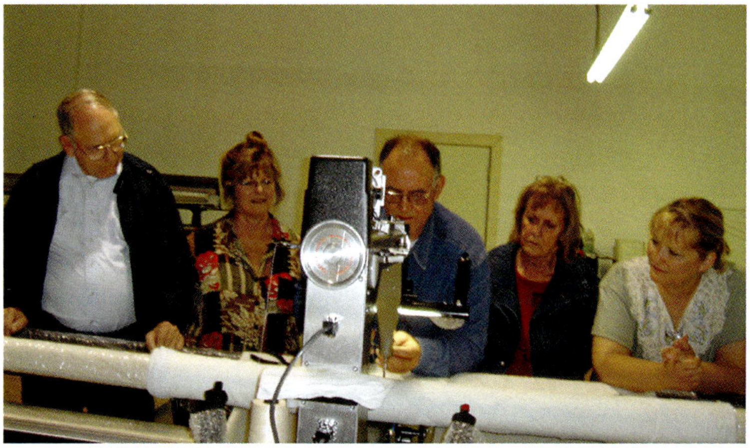

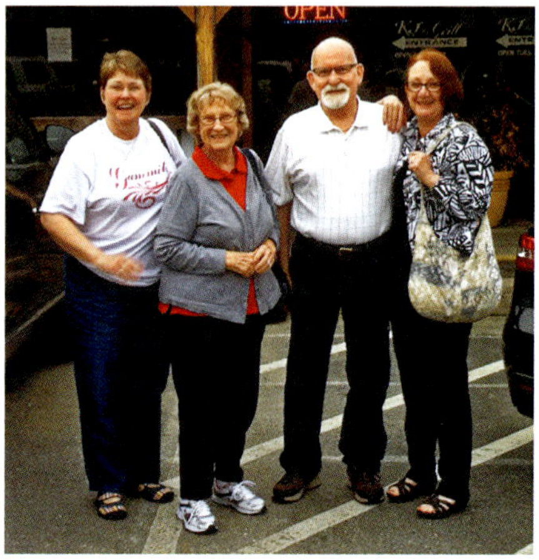
OPEN

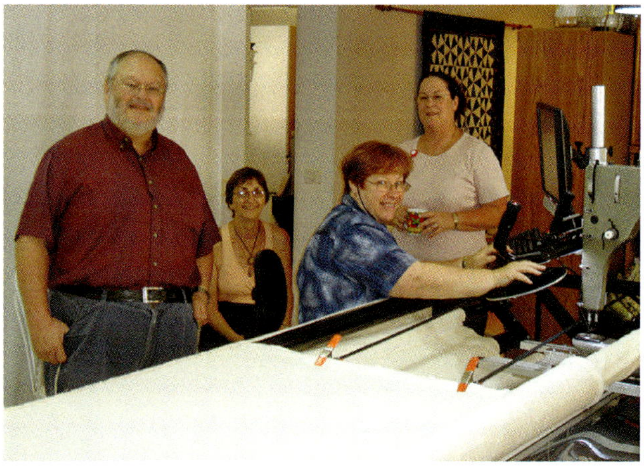

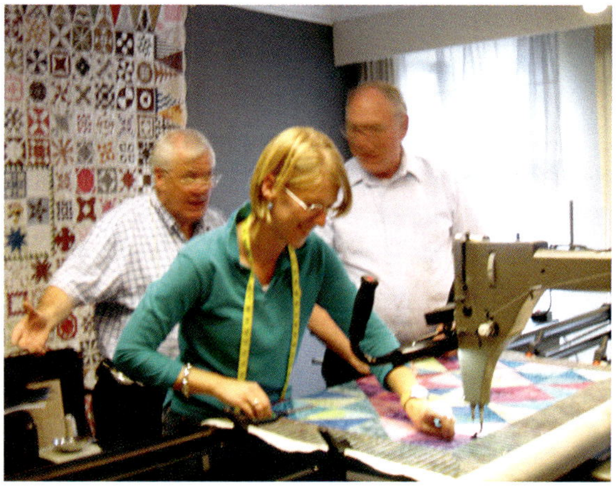

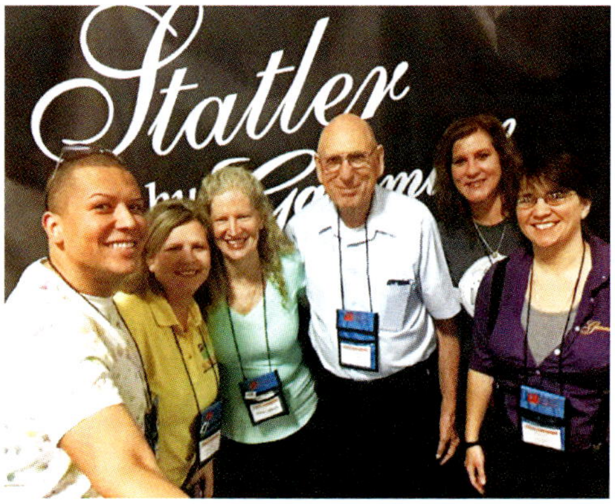
Statler

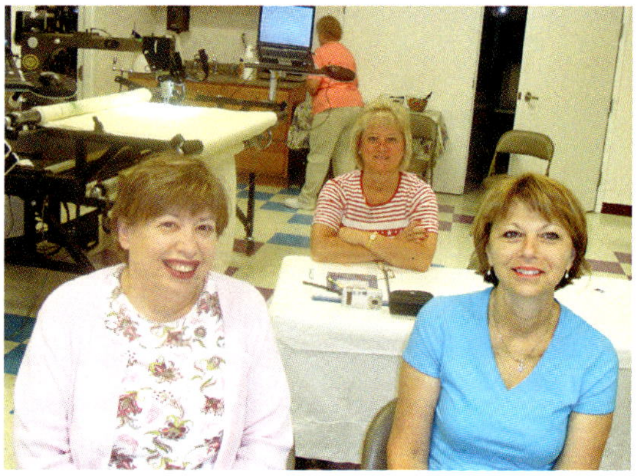

A Touch of Thread Quilting Gallery
Welcomes You To
Statler Stitcher Days 2015

Afterword

Statler Service

There is another Statler pioneer that revolutionized an industry like Paul did. This Statler had many innovations and implemented ideas that forever changed the way hotels are run even today. This pioneer was Ellsworth Milton Statler, founder of the Statler Hotel chain. After designing and building a large temporary hotel for the St. Louis World's Fair of 1904, Ellsworth opened his first permanent hotel in 1907 in Buffalo, New York. It was the first major hotel to have a private bath or shower with running water in every room by implementing what was referred to as the "Statler Plumbing Shaft." He built six more hotels before his untimely death in 1928. His wife continued to head the Hotels Statler Company and oversaw the construction of four additional hotels around the country. In 1954, Conrad Hilton, owner of the Hilton Hotels Company, bought the Statler Company for 111 million dollars, the largest real estate transaction at the time. The last Statler hotel, built in Dallas, Texas, opened in 1956 and was named the Statler-Hilton Hotel.

Ellsworth M. Statler

Hotel Statler - St. Louis, Missouri

Ellsworth's main emphasis above all else was the service provided to his guests. His set of rules to the hotel employees, the "Statler Service Code," became the de facto standard in the hotel industry. His motto of, "The customer is always right" (even if the customer was wrong), garnered more business and success than most other hotels. He was always improving the hotel experience for the guests and modifying room accommodations such as putting telephones in every room, full size closets, lights in every closet, and a hook by the mirror in each bathroom that encouraged guests to reuse their towel, thereby saving laundry costs. He was always improving and a leader in the hotel industry.

Even though Ellsworth and Paul are not directly related (they are 10th cousins, twice removed), and lived in different decades, they both have similar traits and a never-ending enthusiasm in their attempts to always do it better, make it the best, and give support and service to the customer that is second-to-none.   It is what makes both of them very successful and recognized as leaders in their respective businesses and personal lives.

The following quote is from Ellsworth, but Paul could have very well said it himself:

"Life is service. The one who progresses is the one who gives his fellow human being a little more, a little better service."

Old Statler Hotel Postcards

Paul and Mildred riding off to their next adventure